高等学历继续教育学士学位
英语辅导教材

主 审 唐 渠
主 编 周国桥

北京理工大学出版社
BEIJING INSTITUTE OF TECHNOLOGY PRESS

内 容 简 介

本书充分考虑了高等学历继续教育学生的英语学习特征和教学规律，围绕学习需求，将本科阶段所需的英语词汇能力、篇章阅读能力、听说能力和写作能力的训练贯穿于课文学习中。课文涵盖与学生生活密切相关的主题，如"神奇动物""人工智能""运动健身""健康习惯""工作生活""创业""业余生活"和"幽默故事"等，旨在使学生循序渐进地掌握英语基础知识与技能，提高英语应用能力，了解国际社会与文化，增进对不同文化的理解和尊重。同时，为帮助学生熟悉学士学位英语考试，依据考试大纲编写了4套模拟试题，供学生进行考前训练。

全书内容丰富，结构清晰，体例合理，且练习题、模拟题后都配有答案，对参加学位英语考试的学生有切实的帮助。可作为高等学历继续教育非英语专业本科学生的英语教材，也可作各类普通高校非英语专业学生的英语应试工具书，还可供各类英语爱好者自学之用。

版权专有　侵权必究

图书在版编目（CIP）数据

高等学历继续教育学士学位英语辅导教材／周国桥主编. --北京：北京理工大学出版社，2025. 1.
ISBN 978-7-5763-4765-4

Ⅰ. H319.39

中国国家版本馆 CIP 数据核字第 2025Z6L089 号

责任编辑： 武丽娟	**文案编辑：** 武丽娟
责任校对： 刘亚男	**责任印制：** 李志强

出版发行 ／ 北京理工大学出版社有限责任公司
社　　址 ／ 北京市丰台区四合庄路6号
邮　　编 ／ 100070
电　　话 ／ （010）68914026（教材售后服务热线）
　　　　　（010）63726648（课件资源服务热线）
网　　址 ／ http：//www.bitpress.com.cn

版 印 次 ／ 2025年1月第1版第1次印刷
印　　刷 ／ 涿州市新华印刷有限公司
开　　本 ／ 787 mm×1092 mm　1/16
印　　张 ／ 9
字　　数 ／ 209 千字
定　　价 ／ 38.00元

图书出现印装质量问题，请拨打售后服务热线，负责调换

前言

本书依据教育部高等学校大学外语教学指导委员会的《大学英语教学指南》，结合广西壮族自治区高等学历继续教育学士学位英语考试的改革需求，以及国家高等学历继续教育的培养目标和办学特点，专门为接受高等学历继续教育的本科学生而设计。

本书充分考虑了高等学历继续教育学生的英语学习特征和教学规律，围绕学习需求，将本科阶段所需的英语词汇能力、篇章阅读能力、听说能力和写作能力的训练贯穿于课文学习中。同时，为帮助学生熟悉学士学位英语考试，依据考试大纲编写了4套模拟试题，供学生进行考前训练。

在编写过程中，我们以习近平新时代中国特色社会主义思想为指导，致力于使教材具备鲜明的针对性、时代性、思想性、知识性和科学性，突出英语课程的人文性和工具性。在课文学习部分，结合立德树人的教育目标，每章导读引入与党的二十大报告相关的内容，引导大学生明确现代青年的使命与担当。课文涵盖与学生生活密切相关的主题，如"神奇动物""人工智能""运动健身""健康习惯""工作生活""创业""业余生活"和"幽默故事"，使学生循序渐进地掌握英语基础知识与技能，提高英语应用能力，了解国际社会与文化，增进对不同文化的理解和尊重。此外，党的二十大报告中重要概念的中英文表述，有助于加深学生对习近平新时代中国特色社会主义思想的理解。

本书分为五部分，既包括语言基础知识的学习，也涵盖应试技巧的讲解。第一部分为考试大纲；第二部分为课文学习，共8个单元，包括导读、课文学习和语言练习；第三部分是模拟试题，由4套全真模拟测试题组成，每套试题后附有答案详解，方便学生自检自测；第四部分为课文学习的参考答案及译文；第五部分为模拟试题的参考答案。

与其他同类教材相比，本书有以下几个特点：

1. 课文主题生动有趣，在传授语言知识的同时关注价值引领，通过话题导入和课后练习综合考查学生的人文素养。

2. 课文与试题中的素材与时俱进，话题新颖，具有较强的可读性。

3. 全书体现成果导向教育理念，即 OBE 教育理念，教学流程设计遵循启发、赋能、评价的原则。

本书是高等学历继续教育学士学位英语考试的辅导教材，适用于高等学历继续教育非英语专业本科学生的英语学习，也可作为各类英语爱好者学习和训练英语听说读写译技能、系统提高英语水平的工具书。

由于时间仓促和个人水平有限，书中难免存在疏漏或不足之处，恳请各位同行多加指正，提出宝贵意见，以便在今后的修订中改进。

目 录

第一部分 考试大纲 ……………………………………………………………… (1)
  一、总则 …………………………………………………………………………… (1)
  二、评价目标 ……………………………………………………………………… (1)
  三、考试题型 ……………………………………………………………………… (2)

第二部分 课文学习 ……………………………………………………………… (4)
  Unit 1 Fantastic Animals ……………………………………………………… (4)
  Unit 2 Artificial Intelligence ………………………………………………… (10)
  Unit 3 Sports and Fitness …………………………………………………… (17)
  Unit 4 Healthy Habits ………………………………………………………… (23)
  Unit 5 Work and Life ………………………………………………………… (29)
  Unit 6 Starting a Business …………………………………………………… (36)
  Unit 7 Leisure Activities ……………………………………………………… (42)
  Unit 8 Humor and Happiness ………………………………………………… (48)

第三部分 模拟试题 ……………………………………………………………… (56)
  Model Test 1 ………………………………………………………………………… (56)
  Model Test 2 ………………………………………………………………………… (69)
  Model Test 3 ………………………………………………………………………… (82)
  Model Test 4 ………………………………………………………………………… (95)

第四部分 课文学习参考答案及课文译文 …………………………………… (108)
  Unit 1 Fantastic Animals …………………………………………………… (108)
  Unit 2 Artificial Intelligence ………………………………………………… (111)
  Unit 3 Sports and Fitness …………………………………………………… (114)

Unit 4	Healthy Habits	(117)
Unit 5	Work and Life	(120)
Unit 6	Starting a Business	(123)
Unit 7	Leisure Activities	(126)
Unit 8	Humor and Happiness	(129)

第五部分　模拟试题参考答案 (132)

Model Test 1 .... (132)

Model Test 2 .... (133)

Model Test 3 .... (134)

Model Test 4 .... (135)

参考文献 (136)

第一部分　考试大纲

一、总则

为了客观评价高等学历继续教育（非英语专业）学员的英语水平，保证高等学历继续教育毕业生学士学位的授予质量，根据国家高等学历继续教育的培养目标，结合目前高等学历继续教育英语教学的现状和特点以及社会对学生英语能力的实际要求，制定本考试大纲。

本考试为标准化考试。为保证试卷的信度，除写作部分是主观性试题外，其余试题全部是客观性的多项选择题形式。短文写作部分旨在考核考生运用语言的能力，从而提高试卷的效度。

二、评价目标

本考试采用水平测试的方法，旨在考查学生的基本的英语综合应用能力，使他们在今后工作和社会交往中能用英语比较有效地进行信息交流，同时增强其自主学习能力、提高其综合文化素养，以适应我国经济发展和国际交流的需要，并为进一步提高英语水平打下较好的基础。具体要求如下：

（一）词汇

应掌握约 4 000 个英语单词，正确熟练使用由这些单词构成的常用搭配，并具备用构词法识别生词的能力。

（二）语法知识

掌握主谓一致关系，表语从句、宾语从句、定语从句和状语从句等句型，直接引语和间接引语的用法，动词不定式和分词的使用，以及各种时态、主动语态、被动语态等基本语法知识，并注重在语篇层面运用语法知识的能力。

（三）阅读能力

考生应能综合运用英语语言知识和阅读技能，以每分钟 60 词的速度理解各类题材（包括社会生活、人物传记、科普、史地、政治、经济等）和体裁（包括议论文、记叙文、说明文、应用文等）的文字材料。阅读材料的生词量不超过 3%，对于超出教学大纲的生词，应以中文注明词义。

考生能够：

1）掌握所读材料的主旨和大意；

2）了解阐述主旨的事实和细节；

3）根据上下文判断生词或短语的意义；

4）理解单词意义和逻辑关系；

5）进行一定的判断和推理；

6）领会作者的观点和态度。

（四）翻译能力

能在30分钟内根据题目翻译5个句子，语法正确，语言通顺恰当，对源语言和目标语言的翻译准确流畅。

三、考试题型

考试试卷包括4个部分：阅读理解、词汇与语法结构、完形填空、英译汉。全部题目按顺序统一编号，满分为100分，考试时间为120分钟。

第一部分：阅读理解题（Part Ⅰ Reading Comprehension）。共20题，考试时间40分钟。本部分要求考生阅读4篇英文短文，总阅读量不超过1 200词。每篇短文后有5个问题。考生应根据文章内容从每题4个选择项中选出1个最佳答案。

本部分选材的原则是：

1. 题材广泛，包括人物传记、社会、文化、日常知识等，其中所涉及的背景知识均在考生能理解的范围之内；

2. 体裁多样，包括叙述文、说明文、议论文等；

3. 文章的语言难度适中，超出考生应掌握的词汇范围的词，用汉语注明词义。

本部分主要测试以下能力：

1. 掌握所读材料的主旨和大意；

2. 了解说明主旨大意的事实和细节；

3. 既能理解字面意思，也能根据所读材料进行一定的判断和推理；

4. 既能理解个别句子的意思，也能理解上下文的逻辑关系。

本部分的目的是测试考生通过阅读获取信息的能力，既要求准确，也要求有一定的速度。

第二部分：词汇语法题（Part Ⅱ Vocabulary and Structure）。共35题，考试时间30分钟。要求考生从每题4个选择项中选出1个最佳答案。

本部分的目的是测试考生运用词汇、短语及语法结构的能力。

第三部分：完形填空（Part Ⅲ Cloze）。共10题，考试时间20分钟。

给出一篇短文，包含10个填空题，要求考生选择正确单词填空。本部分旨在考查词汇、语法、上下文理解和逻辑推理能力，评估语言运用水平。

第四部分：翻译（Part Ⅳ Translation）。共 5 题，考试时间 30 分钟。

要求考生根据题目翻译 5 个句子。主要考查考生对源语言和目标语言的理解能力，包括语法、词汇运用和表达能力，同时需要对两种语言的文化背景有一定的认识，以确保翻译的准确性和流畅性。

第二部分　课文学习

Unit 1　Fantastic Animals

> 我们坚持绿水青山就是金山银山的理念，坚持山水林田湖草沙一体化保护和系统治理，全方位、全地域、全过程加强生态环境保护，生态文明制度体系更加健全，污染防治攻坚向纵深推进，绿色、循环、低碳发展迈出坚实步伐，生态环境保护发生历史性、转折性、全局性变化，我们的祖国天更蓝、山更绿、水更清。
>
> We have acted on the idea that lucid waters and lush mountains are invaluable assets. We have persisted with a holistic and systematic approach to conserving and improving mountain, water, forest, farmland, grassland, and desert ecosystems, and we have ensured stronger ecological conservation and environmental protection across the board, in all regions, and at all times. China's ecological conservation systems have been improved, the critical battle against pollution has been advanced, and solid progress has been made in promoting green, circular, and low-carbon development. This has led to historic, transformative, and comprehensive changes in ecological and environmental protection and has brought us bluer skies, greener mountains, and cleaner waters.
>
> 习近平《中国共产党第二十次全国代表大会报告》，2022 年 10 月 16 日

Part One
Warming-up Questions

Directions: *Read the following questions and share your answers with your classmates.*

1. If you could send a message in a bottle to the future, what advice would you give the next generation about caring for the planet and its inhabitants?

2. If animals could talk, what do you think they would say to humans about our treatment of them and the natural world?

3. How can we maintain a harmonious coexistence with nature?

4. How can we foster greater respect and appreciation for biodiversity?

5. Have you noticed any significant changes in the natural environment or climate conditions in your hometown in recent years? If so, what kind of changes have you observed?

Useful Words and Expressions

biodiversity 生物多样性	pollution 污染	sustainable 可持续的
habitat 栖息地	optimism 乐观	development 发展
conservation 保护	community 社区	circular economy 循环经济
education 教育	resource 资源	Ecological Civilization 生态文明

Part Two
Text Studies

Our world is filled with an astonishing array of living beings, from the smallest microorganisms to the largest creatures. These plants and animals play vital roles in the delicate balance of our ecosystems, and each one is a testament to the incredible diversity of life on our planet. Let's start our journey to uncover the secrets and marvels of these living beings by exploring the following two articles.

Text A

The Importance of Insects

Insects are everywhere. They are, by far, the most common animals on our planet. More than 1.5 million species of insects have been named. This is three times the number of all other animals **combined**. Their size, shape, color, biology, and life history are so **diverse** that it makes the study of insects absolutely **fascinating**.

Without insects, our lives would be very different. Insects **pollinate** many of our fruits, flowers, and vegetables. We would not have much of the produce that we enjoy and rely on without the pollinating services of insects, not to mention honey, silk, and other useful products that insects provide.

Insects appear to be able to feed on almost kinds of foods. Many insects are omnivorous, meaning that they can eat a number of foods including plants, dead animals, decaying organic matter, and nearly anything they **encounter** in their environment. Still others are specialists in their diet, which means they may rely only on one particular plant or even one specific part of one particular plant to **survive**.

Many insects are **predatory** or **parasitic**, either on plants or on other insects or animals, including people. Such insects are important in nature to help keep pest populations (insects or weeds) at a **tolerable** level. We call this the balance of nature. Predatory and parasitic insects are very valuable when they attack other animals or plants that we consider to be pests.

Insects are very important as **primary** or **secondary** decomposers. Without insects to help break down and dispose of wastes, dead animals and plants would **accumulate** in our environment and it would be messy indeed.

Insects also play an important role in the food web. They are the sole food source for many birds and animals. Insects themselves are harvested and eaten by people in some cultures. They are a rich source of protein, vitamins, and minerals.

And insects make our world much more interesting. Naturalists **derive** a great deal of satisfaction in watching ants work, bees pollinate, or dragonflies hunt. Can you imagine how uninteresting life would become without having butterflies or lightning beetles to add interest to a **landscape**? People benefit in so many ways by sharing their world with insects.

New Words

combine /kəmˈbaɪn/ v.	结合
diverse /daɪˈvɜːrs/ adj.	多样的
fascinating /ˈfæsɪneɪtɪŋ/ adj.	迷人的
pollinate /ˈpɒlɪneɪt/ v.	传粉
encounter /ɪnˈkaʊntər/ v.	遭遇，遇到
survive /səˈvaɪv/ v.	生存
predatory /ˈpredətəri/ adj.	捕食性的
parasitic /pærəˈsɪtɪk/ adj.	寄生的
tolerable /ˈtɒlərəbl/ adj.	可接受的，能容忍的
primary /ˈpraɪməri/ adj.	主要的
secondary /ˈsekəndəri/ adj.	次要的
accumulate /əˈkjuːmjəleɪt/ v.	积累
derive /dɪˈraɪv/ v.	获得
landscape /ˈlæn(d)ʃkeɪp/ n.	风景

Phrases and Expressions

by far	迄今为止
more than	超过，多于
so...that...	如此……以至于……
rely on	依赖于，依靠
appear to	看起来，似乎
either...or...	要么……要么……

play an important role in…	在………中扮演重要角色
a great deal of	大量的
share…with…	与……分享

Cultural Notes

predatory vs. parasitic	它们的名词分别为 predation（捕食）和 parasitism（寄生）。寄生（parasitism）是一种生物（寄生虫）生活在另一种生物（宿主）的体内或体表，对其造成某种伤害，并在生理结构上适应这种生活方式。捕食（predation）是一种生物（捕食者）捕获并吃掉另一种生物（猎物）

Exercises

Ⅰ. Understanding the text

Directions: *Answer the following questions according to the text.*

1. What is the most common type of animal on our planet?
_____

2. How many species of insects have been named?
_____

3. What is the term used to describe insects that can eat a number of foods?
_____

4. What is the role of predatory and parasitic insects in nature?
_____

5. How do naturalists benefit from the presence of insects?
_____

Ⅱ. Vocabulary and phrases

Directions: *Fill in the blanks with the words given below. Change the form where necessary. Each word can be used only once.*

combine	derive	accumulate	tolerate	survive
encounter	landscape	primary	diverse	fascinating

1. The two companies will _____ their resources to enhance their market presence.

2. The _____ interests of the club members make it difficult to plan activities.

3. Travelers may _____ different cultures and traditions when visiting new coun-

tries.

4. The wild animals _____ the wildfire, but their habitat was damaged.

5. Education is a _____ focus for the government this year.

6. The _____ of data will help researchers understand the phenomenon.

7. I find the study of space and the universe to be truly _____ .

8. His performance was _____, but he knew he could do much better.

9. The company _____ its profits from a variety of sources.

10. The _____ of the countryside was amazing.

Ⅲ. Translation

Directions: *Translate the following sentences into Chinese.*

1. Their size, shape, color, biology, and life history are so diverse that it makes the study of insects absolutely fascinating.

_____

2. Insects pollinate many of our fruits, flowers, and vegetables.

_____

3. Such insects are important in nature to help keep pest populations (insects or weeds) at a tolerable level.

_____

4. Insects themselves are harvested and eaten by people in some cultures. They are a rich source of protein, vitamins, and minerals.

_____

5. People benefit in so many ways by sharing their world with insects.

_____

Ⅳ. Writing

Directions: *Endangered species play an important role in maintaining the balance of ecosystems, therefore, it is essential to protect their habitats. Please write an essay on "How can we protect the habitats of endangered species?" with no less than 100 words.*

Text B

The Deep Culture of Elephants

Elephants have not only amazing physical features but also a rich cultural history. This history is passed down through their customs and social behaviors, which younger elephants learn, remember, and share with their herd. These behaviors are important for their survival and well-being.

This learning happens partly because of their special social structure. Elephants live in close groups made up of many generations, led by older females called matriarchs. The younger elephants watch and copy the older ones, learning from their experiences. The whole herd does almost everything together, like finding food, eating, and taking care of each other's young. These activities create strong relationships that can last many years, even decades.

Because of these strong bonds, elephants seem to have feelings, just like humans. They have been seen showing sadness when one of them dies. When an elephant passes away, the other elephants often return to the place where it died. This behavior seems to be part of their way to mourn. They may smell and touch the body and cover the area with leaves. A 2020 study found that "elephants show interest in their dead, no matter their past relationships". This suggests that elephants have a high level of awareness and understanding.

There is a saying in many languages: "an elephant never forgets". In fact, elephants' good memory has been important for the survival of some groups. A study in the Great Kruger National Park found that during a severe drought in 2016, groups led by older female elephants who had experienced drought before had higher survival rates.

So, consider yourself lucky to share the planet with these large and wonderful animals.

Exercises

I. **Understanding the text**.

Directions: *Read the above text carefully and choose the best answer to each question.*

1. What is one way younger elephants learn from older elephants?

A) By listening to stories.

B) By watching and copying their behaviors.

C) By playing games.

D) By exploring alone.

2. Who leads the elephant herd?

A) Younger males.

B) Older females.

C) Younger females.

D) Adult males.

3. How do elephants show their feelings when another elephant dies?

A) They become aggressive.

B) They ignore the death.

C) They show sadness and return to the spot.

D) They celebrate.

4. What does the saying "an elephant never forgets" suggest about elephants?

A) They forget easily.

B) They have a good memory.

C) They have no emotions.

D) They are not social animals.

5. Why is the study in the Great Kruger National Park significant?

A) It shows elephants can swim.

B) It reveals elephants have strong bonds.

C) It indicates older elephants help groups survive during droughts.

D) It proves elephants are endangered.

Ⅱ. **Translation**

Directions: *Translate the following sentences from the text into Chinese.*

1. Elephants learn from the experiences of older elephants.

2. The whole herd does almost everything together.

3. When an elephant dies, the others often return to the spot.

4. Elephants have strong bonds that can last for many years.

5. A study found that older elephants help groups survive during droughts.

Unit 2　Artificial Intelligence

巩固优势产业领先地位，在关系安全发展的领域加快补齐短板，提升战略性资源供应保障能力。推动战略性新兴产业融合集群发展，构建新一代信息技术、人工智能、生物技术、新能源、新材料、高端装备、绿色环保等一批新的增长引擎。

We will consolidate our leading position in industries where we excel, work faster to shore up weaknesses in sectors vital to China's development security, and improve our capacity for securing the supply of strategic resources. We will promote the integrated and clustered development of strategic emerging industries and cultivate new growth engines such as next‐generation information technology, artificial intelligence, biotechnology, new energy, new materials, high‐end equipment, and green industry.

习近平《中国共产党第二十次全国代表大会报告》，2022年10月16日

Part One
Warming-up Questions

Directions: *Read the following questions and share your answers with your classmates.*

1. How often do you use the face recognition function on your smartphones?
2. What do you think of self-driving cars? Are they safe?
3. What are potential benefits of more AI in daily life?
4. How could AI impact future job markets?
5. What ethical concerns arise from AI in daily life?

Useful Words and Expressions

technology 技术	algorithm 算法	sensors 传感器
navigation 导航	collision 碰撞	application 应用
limitations 局限性	unexpected 意外的	automation 自动化
facial recognition 人脸识别	employment 就业	adaptation 适应

Part Two
Text Studies

AI has become a part of our daily lives, even though we may not realize it. AI powers many of the devices and technologies we use every day, from our phones to our computers. It helps us make decisions, plan our days, and find information without much thought. Let's gain a deeper understanding of how AI is shaping our life by reading the following articles.

Text A

Impacts of Artificial Intelligence on Our Everyday Life

In today's fast-paced world, technology, especially **artificial intelligence** (AI), has become a big part of our daily lives. From the moment we wake up to the time we lay our heads to rest, AI is quietly working behind the scenes to make our daily experiences **smoother**, smarter, and more enjoyable.

AI technologies can simplify our everyday tasks, making our daily **routines** more efficient and convenient. AI-powered **virtual** assistants can manage our **calendars**, schedule appointments, set **reminders**, and organize our to-do lists. With natural language processing and machine learning capabilities, these assistants understand our **preferences** and adapt to our needs, ensuring us stay on top of our tasks effortlessly.

In healthcare, AI is making a big difference. **Wearable** devices with AI can monitor our health, track our activity, and even predict potential issues. Telemedicine **platforms** use AI to offer remote doctor consultations, so we can get medical help without going to a clinic.

AI also improves communication. Email apps use AI to sort our messages and **prioritize** our inboxes. Chatbots on websites and social media platforms offer **instant** customer support, answering queries and resolving issues promptly. AI-powered language translation tools enable us to bridge communication gaps between people no matter the language that is spoken.

Additionally, AI is contributing to creative work. Photo editing applications use AI algorithms to enhance images, suggesting edits that align with our aesthetic preferences. Music **composition** tools can **generate** songs based on our input, inspiring musicians and amateurs alike to explore new artistic horizons. These innovations **empower** individuals to express themselves creatively with AI as a **collaborative** partner.

As AI continues to make progress, its **potential** to improve our daily lives is growing. Smart homes with AI-driven systems can adjust lighting, temperature, and safety. **Autonomous** vehicles promise safer and more **efficient** commuting. Predictive analytics can **optimize** supply chains.

The **integration** of AI into our daily lives is not just a trend—it's a major change in how we interact with technology. By making tasks easier, personalizing experiences, revolutionizing healthcare, enhancing communication, and fueling creativity, AI is opening the door to a more convenient, efficient, and tailored way of living. As we embrace AI's **transformative** power, it's important to use it responsibly, ensuring it benefits society as a whole.

New Words

artificial /ˌɑːtɪˈfɪʃəl/ adj.	人工的
intelligence /ɪnˈtelɪdʒəns/ n.	智慧，智力
smooth /smuːð/ adj.	顺利的，平滑的
routine /ruːˈtiːn/ n.	日常
virtual /ˈvɜːrtʃuəl/ adj.	虚拟的
calendar /ˈkælɪndər/ n.	日历
reminder /rɪˈmaɪndər/ n.	提醒
preference /ˈprɛfərəns/ n.	偏好
wearable /ˈwɛrəbəl/ adj.	可穿戴的
platform /ˈplætˌfɔːrm/ n.	平台
prioritize /praɪˈɒrɪˌtaɪz/ v.	优先排序
instant /ˈɪnstənt/ adj.	即时的
composition /ˌkɒmpəˈzɪʃn/ n.	作曲
generate /ˈdʒenəreɪt/ v.	生成

empower /ɪmˈpaʊər/ v. 赋予权力
collaborative /kəˈlæbərətɪv/ adj. 协作的
potential /pəˈtenʃəl/ n. 潜力
autonomous /ɔːˈtɒnəməs/ adj. 自主的
efficient /ɪˈfɪʃnt/ adj. 高效的
optimize /ˈɒptɪˌmaɪz/ v. 优化
integration /ˌɪntɪˈɡreɪʃn/ n. 整合
transformative /trænzˈfɔːrmətɪv/ adj. 变革性的

Phrases

adapt to 适应
be tailored to 专门针对……
align with 与……一致
interact with 与……互动
contribute to 有助于……

Cultural Notes

| supply chain | 供应链是由一连串供应商和采购商组成的团队,以接力赛团队的模式,完成从采购原材料,到制成中间产品及至最终产品,然后将最终产品交付用户为功能的,由一系列设施和分布选择形成的网络 |

Exercises

Ⅰ. Understanding the text

Directions: Answer the following questions according to the text.

1. What are the ways AI helps make our routine tasks simpler?

2. How do AI-powered virtual assistants assist us?

3. In healthcare, what can AI-powered wearable devices do?

4. In what ways is AI contributing to creative work?

5. What is important as we embrace AI's transformative power?

Ⅱ. Vocabulary and phrases

Directions: *Fill in the blanks with the words given below. Change the form where necessary. Each word can be used only once.*

| smooth | wearable | optimize | virtual | generate |
| preference | efficient | instant | adapt | contribute |

1. The company uses advanced analytics to _____ their supply chain operations and improve efficiency.

2. The _____ environment created by the augmented reality app felt incredibly realistic.

3. After some adjustments, the software update provided a much _____ user experience.

4. The AI-powered system can _____ personalized content recommendations based on the user's browsing history.

5. _____ devices can provide real-time health data, making it easier to stay fit.

6. The team's collaborative efforts _____ to the successful completion of the project.

7. The market research team analyzed customer _____ to inform the product development strategy.

8. Successful leaders must be able to _____ to new challenges and uncertainties in the workplace.

9. Employees who work in a/an _____ work environment tend to be more productive and engaged.

10. The _____ messaging app allows users to communicate in real-time.

Ⅲ. Translation

Directions: *Translate the following sentences into Chinese.*

1. Wearable devices with AI can monitor our health, track our activity, and even predict potential issues.

_____

2. Telemedicine platforms use AI to offer remote doctor consultations, so we can get medical help without going to a clinic.

_____

3. Email apps use AI to sort our messages and prioritize our inboxes.

_____

4. Photo editing applications use AI algorithms to enhance images, suggesting edits that align

with our aesthetic preferences.

5. As AI continues to make progress, its potential to improve our daily lives is growing.

Ⅳ. Writing

Directions: *The rapid development of AI-powered robots has sparked concerns that machines may one day surpass human intelligence. However, others argue the human mind will always be superior, as machines are limited to their programming. What is your view on artificial intelligence in the future? Please write an essay based on the above questions with no less than 100 words.*

Text B

A Day in the Life of AI

Artificial Intelligence (AI) has become deeply integrated into our daily lives. From the mobile phones we use upon waking, to the electric car we drive to work, to the hospital where we are employed, AI is playing a role.

At 7 a.m., you glance at your mobile phone, which unlocks using Face ID. This AI system tracks changes in your appearance over time, updating its authentication model accordingly. The phone's camera app also utilizes computer vision to recognize people and objects, categorizing images. Celia, the voice assistant, leverages natural language processing and machine learning to interpret your spoken commands.

At 7:40 a.m., you ask Celia to play music. Celia sends your voice recording to Amazon's servers, where speech recognition software converts the audio to text. Language processing algorithms then extract the meaning, and the response is beamed back to your device. Celia's learning process involves human review of sample requests to continuously improve its capabilities.

At 8:10 a.m., you drive to work in your Xiaomi SU7. The car's AI system collects data from eight cameras, identifies obstacles, lanes, intersections, and traffic signals, and makes the appropriate maneuvers. However, these self-driving cars are limited to handling only the situations they have encountered before, struggling with rare or unexpected events.

Arriving at the hospital by 9 a.m., you see that the medical field is heavily investing in AI research and applications, from scan analysis to precision surgery. A lung health screening program uses AI-based computer-aided detection to assist in identifying lung nodules, with final diagnosis made by physicians.

During your lunch break, you help your daughter refine her job application letter. AI is transforming the hiring process, with applicants using AI tools to craft personalized cover letters, and companies employing AI algorithms to screen and score candidates.

Throughout your day, the influence of artificial intelligence is ubiquitous, reshaping various aspects of our daily lives. While the technology still has limitations, AI has become an indispensable part of how we live, work, and interact.

Exercises

Ⅰ. **Understanding the text**.

Directions: *Answer the following questions according to the text.*

1. What does the mobile phone's Face ID do?

2. How does Celia work to understand user commands?

3. What can Xiaomi SU7's self-driving system do?

4. What is the focus of the medical field's AI investments?

5. How is AI transforming the hiring process?

Ⅱ. **Translation**

Directions: *Translate the following sentences from the text into Chinese.*

1. Artificial Intelligence (AI) has become deeply integrated into our daily lives.

2. This AI system tracks changes in your appearance over time, updating its authentication model accordingly.

3. Celia, the voice assistant, leverages natural language processing and machine learning to interpret your spoken commands.

4. The medical field is heavily investing in AI research and applications, from scan analysis to precision surgery.

5. The influence of artificial intelligence is ubiquitous, reshaping various aspects of our daily lives.

Unit 3　Sports and Fitness

> 坚持以文塑旅、以旅彰文，推进文化和旅游深度融合发展。广泛开展全民健身活动，加强青少年体育工作，促进群众体育和竞技体育全面发展，加快建设体育强国。
>
> We will encourage positive interplay between culture and tourism and advance deeper integration of the two sectors. We will launch extensive public fitness initiatives, improve physical education for our young people, promote all-around development of recreational and competitive sports, and move faster to build China into a country strong in sports.
>
> 习近平《中国共产党第二十次全国代表大会报告》，2022 年 10 月 16 日

Part One
Warming-up Questions

Directions：*Read the following questions and share your answers with your classmates.*

1. What are the benefits of playing team sports versus individual sports? Which type of sport do you prefer and why?

2. Should professional athletes be considered role models for young people? What responsibilities come with that status?

3. What are the challenges or barriers that prevent people from exercising regularly, and how can these be overcome?

4. Have you watched any sports live at a sports ground or stadium? How was the experience? Was it better than watching on TV?

5. What are some key achievements of Chinese athletes in the Olympics?

Useful Words and Expressions

ballet 芭蕾舞	breakdancing 霹雳舞	boxing 拳击
cycling 骑自行车	fencing 击剑	hiking 徒步旅行
martial arts 武术	tennis 网球	volleyball 排球
strength 力量	competition 竞争	persistence 坚持

Part Two
Text Studies

Physical activity and sports play a crucial role in maintaining our overall health and well-being. Regular exercise can strengthen the cardiovascular system, improve muscle tone and flexibility, boost mood and energy levels, and reduce the risk of chronic diseases. Let's explore the following articles to uncover more potential benefits we can gain from participating in sports.

Text A

Is There a Best Time to Exercise?

With our already busy lives, finding time to exercise can feel like one more thing on our "to do" list. So maybe it would help if there was "a best time" to **exercise**? Could exercising at certain times help **maximize** our fitness goals? The answer is "yes", but it's easier than you think—no matter who you are, or when you like to work out.

There are clear **benefits** to exercising in the morning. Many of us have more free time compared to later in the day, and it may therefore be easier for us to stick to a morning workout routine. A study **published** in Medicine and Science in Sports and Exercise found that **participants** who exercised in the morning, increased their **physical** activity throughout the day, were less **distracted** by food, and slept better. Exercising on an empty **stomach** before breakfast could also burn more fat and increase **metabolism**, which means you'll continue to burn **calories** throughout the day.

So, good news for early birds, but what if you're not a morning person? Working out in the afternoon or evening also has benefits, just **different** ones. For example, your body's ability to perform **peaks** in the afternoon, according to a 2010 study by the Scandinavian Journal of Medicine and Science in Sports. Also, in the afternoon and evening, your reaction time is quickest, and your heart **rate** and blood **pressure** are lowest, which reduce your chance of **injury** while improving performance.

But does any of this change depending on whether you're a man or a woman? Our bodies are different, after all, so the best time to exercise may be different too. A 2022 study looked at **exactly** this question and the **results** showed that there are some differences. For women who want to **reduce** blood pressure, morning exercise proved more beneficial. In contrast, for men aiming to **improve** heart health, the evening seems to be the better time. However, the overall finding of the study was that both genders can accrue clear advantages by exercising at either time of day.

So what time is best? It seems the answer is: whatever time is best for you!

New Words

exercise /ˈeksərsaɪz/ v.	运动
maximize /ˈmæksɪmaɪz/ v.	使最大化，充分利用
benefit /ˈbenɪfɪt/ n.	利益，好处
publish /ˈpʌblɪʃ/ v.	出版，发表
participant /pɑrˈtɪsəpənt/ n.	参与者，参加者
physical /ˈfɪzɪkəl/ adj.	身体的，物理的
distract /dɪˈstrækt/ v.	分散注意力，使心烦意乱

stomach /ˈstʌmək/	n.	胃，腹部
metabolism /məˈtæbəlɪzəm/	n.	新陈代谢
calories /ˈkæləriːz/	n.	卡路里
different /ˈdɪfərənt/	adj.	不同的，差异的
peak /piːk/	n.	峰值，顶点
rate /reɪt/	n.	比率，速度
pressure /ˈpreʃər/	n.	压力
injury /ˈɪndʒəri/	n.	伤害，损伤
exactly /ɪgˈzæktli/	adv.	正好，精确地
result /rɪˈzʌlt/	n.	结果
reduce /rɪˈduːs/	v.	减少，降低
improve /ɪmˈpruːv/	v.	改善，提高

Phrases

work out	锻炼，运动
compared to	相比于
stick to	坚持，持续
depend on	依赖于，取决于
after all	毕竟，终究

Cultural Notes

metabolism	新陈代谢。它是指生物体内各种化学反应的过程，包括同化作用和异化作用。影响新陈代谢的因素有年龄、性别、肌肉量、激素水平、温度、饮食等。通过适当的运动、合理的饮食，可以提高新陈代谢的速率，从而达到健康、减重的目的

Exercises

Ⅰ. **Understanding the text**

Directions：*Answer the following questions according to the text.*

1. What are the benefits of exercising in the morning?

2. When does the body's ability to give the best performance according to the 2010 study?

3. How can exercising in the afternoon or evening help reduce the risk of injury?
_____

4. How do the results of the 2022 study show that the best time to exercise may be different for men and women?
_____

5. What is the ultimate conclusion about the best time to exercise?
_____

Ⅱ. Vocabulary and phrases

Directions: *Fill in the blanks with the words given below. Change the form where necessary. Each word can be used only once.*

| exact | maximize | benefit | peak | participant |
| pressure | distract | physical | compare | stick |

1. The company's goal is to _____ the benefits of the new investment strategy.

2. _____ to living in the city, living in the countryside is generally quieter and more peaceful.

3. The _____ reasons for the project's delay were not immediately clear.

4. She reached the _____ of her career when she was awarded the prestigious industry honor.

5. The _____ of the employee wellness program have been numerous, including increased productivity and reduced healthcare costs.

6. Each _____ in the study was asked to complete a detailed questionnaire about their habits.

7. She felt a lot of _____ to perform well on the exam, leading her to study late into the night.

8. Exercise program can have positive effects on both our mental and _____ well-being.

9. The team leader reminded the group to avoid _____ and stay on task to meet the tight deadline.

10. It's important to _____ to the company's core values and not deviate from them, even in challenging times.

Ⅲ. Translation

Directions: *Translate the following sentences into Chinese.*

1. Many of us have more free time compared to later in the day, and it may therefore be easier for us to stick to a morning workout routine.

2. Exercising on an empty stomach before breakfast could also burn more fat and increase metabolism, which means you'll continue to burn calories throughout the day.

3. Also, in the afternoon and evening, your reaction time is quickest, and your heart rate and blood pressure are lowest, which reduce your chance of injury while improving performance.

4. For women who want to reduce blood pressure, morning exercise proved more beneficial.

5. However, the overall finding of the study was that both genders can accrue clear advantages by exercising at either time of day.

Ⅳ. **Writing**

Directions: *Nowadays, more and more people are using fitness trackers and apps to record their exercise activities. What is the role of fitness trackers and apps in health management? Please write an essay based on the above question with no less than 100 words.*

Text B

Is Watching Sports Good for Your Well-being?

If you're a sports fan, you may be familiar with the emotional roller coaster that comes with being a sports spectator. Whether you're part of a buzzing crowd in a stadium, or just watching at home on TV, it's easy to get caught up in the highs and the lows when you celebrate or commiserate with your favourite team or athlete. In fact, a study from Croatia has even shown that the emotional stress experienced during a football match can increase the risk of cardiovascular incidents. However, the question remains—can watching sports also have positive effects on one's well-being?

The evidence suggests that people who watch live sporting events experience greater well-being than those who don't. A study conducted by the Anglia Ruskin University in the UK found that sports spectators felt less lonely and had higher levels of life satisfaction. According to the study, watching live sport of all types provides many opportunities for social interaction and this helps to forge group identity and belonging. This social engagement ultimately reduces feelings of loneliness and enhances overall well-being.

But, if for any reason you aren't keen on going to live events, don't worry! Watching sports on TV or on the internet may also have positive effects, according to a 2021 study. They found that older adults who watched sports were less likely to have depressive symptoms than those who didn't. Additionally, the study revealed that sports spectators tended to have more extensive social networks than non-spectators. The authors of this research suggest that the social connections and interactions fostered through sports viewing may contribute to a lower risk of developing depressive symptoms.

So, the cheers at a live sports event or even casual chit-chat with friends about your favourite team can bring a sense of camaraderie and may reduce loneliness and depression. It seems the health benefits of sports are not limited to physical activity through participation in them, but that we can make gains in our general well-being through social bonding.

Exercises

Ⅰ. Understanding the text.

Directions: *Answer the following questions according to the text.*

1. According to the research findings, how can watching sports events impact cardiovascular health?

2. The study results showed that people who watch live sporting events have a better experience in what aspects compared to those who don't?

3. Apart from live attendance, how can watching sports on TV or online also provide benefits?

4. According to the research, how can watching sports events potentially impact the viewers' social networks?

5. Overall, what kind of impact do you think watching sports events can have on people's physical and mental well-being?

Ⅱ. Translation

Directions: *Translate the following sentences from the text into Chinese.*

1. If you're a sports fan, you may be familiar with the emotional roller coaster that comes with being a sports spectator.

2. The evidence suggests that people who watch live sporting events experience greater well-being than those who don't.

3. According to the study, watching live sport of all types provides many opportunities for social interaction and this helps to forge group identity and belonging.

4. The authors of this research suggest that the social connections and interactions fostered

through sports viewing may contribute to a lower risk of developing depressive symptoms.

5. It seems the health benefits of sports are not limited to physical activity through participation in them, but that we can make gains in our general well-being through social bonding.

Unit 4　Healthy Habits

> 人民健康是民族昌盛和国家强盛的重要标志。把保障人民健康放在优先发展的战略位置，完善人民健康促进政策。重视心理健康和精神卫生。促进中医药传承创新发展。深入开展健康中国行动和爱国卫生运动，倡导文明健康生活方式。
>
> People's health is a key indicator of a prosperous nation and a strong country. We must give strategic priority to ensuring the people's health and improve policies on promoting public health. We will place importance on mental and psychological health. We will promote the preservation and innovative development of traditional Chinese medicine. We will further advance the Healthy China Initiative and patriotic health campaigns and promote sound, healthy lifestyles.
>
> 习近平《中国共产党第二十次全国代表大会报告》，2022 年 10 月 16 日

Part One
Warming-up Questions

Directions: Read the following questions and share your answers with your classmates.

1. What are some simple daily habits that can make a big difference in leading a healthier life?

2. How can we build healthy habits as a family or community, and support each other in the process?

3. How can we maintain a healthy lifestyle while managing a busy work or school schedule?

4. What are the benefits of trying new forms of physical activity and stepping out of our comfort zones?

5. What kinds of public awareness campaigns and education programs has China implemented to encourage healthier behaviors?

Useful Words and Expressions

habit 习惯	community 社区	lifestyle 生活方式
schedule 日程	comfort zone 舒适区	campaign 活动
nutrition 营养	flexibility 灵活性	endurance 耐力
meditation 冥想	immunity 免疫力	outdoor recreation 户外休闲

Part Two
Text Studies

Living a healthy lifestyle is essential for optimal physical, mental, and social well-being. Regular exercise, balanced nutrition, and effective stress management are key. A healthy lifestyle also benefits social connections and the environment. Let's explore articles to know more about how to enhance our quality of life.

Text A

Houseplants: Good or Bad?

There's no place like home. It's the place where we're **surrounded** by our **possessions** and creature comforts. We **purchase** things to give our homes a personal touch and create a certain **atmosphere**. One thing we're buying more of is houseplants. But are these "living" additions to our homes good for us and the environment?

Houseplants, also known as pot plants, are **popular** on social media; add a natural touch and they have the ability to brighten up a room without costing much. A study found that nearly 72% of adults in the UK had a houseplant in their home, with this **figure** rising to 80% of 16-24 year olds. A fifth of owners also said they use plants in the home to **boost** their health and well-being. Plant sales last year were up on the **previous** year.

It seems millennials are driving the growth in the sales of houseplants. According to research, more young people are living in **flats** without a garden. 24 year-old Daisy Hale said that "being able to care for something but not having too much **commitment** is ideal for my lifestyle."

There are many types of houseplants, from hanging baskets to **cacti** and **ferns**. They are easy to care for, and there have been unproven claims that they improve the air **quality** in our home. But whatever their benefits, there are now **concerns** that they might not be so good for the environment. Some are bought online and shipped from overseas. Buying houseplants that are shipped from far-away locations can be harmful to the environment. The further the plants have to travel, whether by air, sea, or land, the greater the **carbon** footprint and negative impact.

But botanist James Wong argues that home delivery has less of an environmental impact than **multiple** trips to the garden centre in a car. Although he's not too concerned about the environmental impact, others are worried about the **plastic** pots they are in and the type of peat that some of them are grown in. However, a **sustainable** approach to buying them may be the best way forward if we want to introduce some natural greenery into our homes.

New Words

surround /səˈraʊnd/ v.	包围
possession /pəˈzeʃ(ə)n/ n.	所有物，财产
purchase /ˈpɜːtʃɪs/ v.	购买
atmosphere /ˈætməsfɪə/ n.	气氛
popular /ˈpɒpjʊlə/ adj.	流行的
figure /ˈfɪɡə/ n.	数字
boost /buːst/ v.	提高
previous /ˈpriːviəs/ adj.	以前的
flat /flæt/ n.	公寓
commitment /kəˈmɪtmənt/ n.	承诺
cacti /ˈkæktaɪ/ n.	仙人掌（复数）
ferns /fɜːnz/ n.	蕨类植物（复数）
quality /ˈkwɒlɪti/ n.	质量
concern /kənˈsɜːn/ n.	关心，顾虑
carbon /ˈkɑːbən/ n.	碳
multiple /ˈmʌltɪpl/ adj.	多种的
plastic /ˈplæstɪk/ adj.	塑料制的
sustainable /səˈsteɪnəbl/ adj.	可持续的

Phrases

brighten up	使……变得明亮
according to	根据
be able to	能够
care for	照顾
be harmful to	对……有害
be worried about	担心
introduce…into…	引入……到……

Cultural Notes

millennials	千禧一代，是指出生于 20 世纪且 20 世纪时未成年，在跨入 21 世纪（即 2000 年）以后达到成年年龄的一代人。这一代人在成长过程中广泛接触和使用了互联网、社交媒体等新兴技术。与上一代人相比，千禧一代更关注社会责任、环境保护等议题

Exercises

Ⅰ. Understanding the text

Directions: *Answer the following questions according to the text.*

1. How many adults in the UK had a houseplant in their home according to the Royal Horticultural Society?

2. What is the main reason why millennials are driving the growth in the sales of houseplants?

3. What is the concern regarding buying houseplants that are shipped from overseas?

4. What are the specific concerns that others have about the environmental impact of houseplants?

5. What is the main reason why the passage suggests that a sustainable approach may be the best way to introduce natural greenery into our homes?

Ⅱ. Vocabulary and phrases

Directions: *Fill in the blanks with the words given below. Change the form where necessary. Each word can be used only once.*

boost	purchase	quality	plastic	concern
surround	commitment	atmosphere	multiple	brighten

1. The beautiful mountains _____ the small village, providing a picturesque backdrop.

2. After saving for months, I finally made a decision of _____ my dream bicycle.

3. Maintaining a healthy lifestyle requires dedication and a strong _____ .

4. Positive customer reviews can _____ a company's reputation and credibility.

5. Maintaining _____ control is crucial in the manufacturing process.

6. The medical team listened carefully to the patient's _____ about their treatment

plan.

7. The project required _____ revisions before it was finally approved.

8. The restaurant had a cozy _____ that made it perfect for a romantic dinner.

9. Recycling _____ waste is an important step towards a more sustainable future.

10. Listening to music always helps to _____ my mood.

Ⅲ. Translation

Directions: *Translate the following sentences into Chinese.*

1. It's the place where we're surrounded by our possessions and creature comforts.

_____

2. But are these "living" additions to our homes good for us and the environment?

_____

3. Buying houseplants that are shipped from far-away locations can be harmful to the environment.

_____

4. The further the plants have to travel, whether by air, sea, or land, the greater the carbon footprint and negative impact.

_____

5. Home delivery has less of an environmental impact than multiple trips to the garden centre in a car.

_____

Ⅳ. Writing

Directions: *What are the differences between urban and rural lifestyles? What are their respective characteristics? How do you view these two ways of living? Please write an essay based on the above questions with no less than 100 words.*

Text B

The Dangers of Sitting

Did you know many adults sit down for more than nine hours a day—maybe you're one of them! Whether it's working at a desk, sitting motionless in a car, bus or train or lounging on the sofa watching TV, we have a much more sedentary lifestyle than our parents and grandparents did. The question that this raises is just what is it doing to our bodies?

The news is not good. A study done in the 1950s compared bus drivers with the ticket collectors, who walked around the bus selling tickets. It showed that drivers, who spent many hours sitting at the wheel, were twice as likely to have heart attacks than the more active ticket collectors. In fact, sitting for a long time has been linked to a number of different health problems, even in people who otherwise exercise regularly. If you sit all day, you burn far fewer calories than someone with a more active job. There is evidence that it slows your metabolism and makes it harder for your body to control blood sugar levels, increasing the risk of diabetes.

One possible answer to this problem is for desk workers to use standing desks, to spend at least part of their day on their feet. One small study showed that office workers who stood for three hours after lunch had a much smaller increase in blood sugar levels, while another suggested that by standing for three or four hours a day over the period of a year, people would burn as many calories as if they had run ten marathons.

Other experts question this figure and point out that standing all day can also have negative impacts, such as leg or back pain. They recommend that if people do use standing desks, they should gradually increase the amount of time they spend on their feet. They also point out that there are many alternatives to sitting, and that their impact is unlikely to be the same: walking, for example, burns far more calories than standing.

Exercises

I. Understanding the text.

Directions: *Answer the following questions according to the text.*

1. What are some of the common sedentary activities mentioned in the passage?

2. What was the key finding of the 1950s study?

3. What is one possible solution to the problem of excessive sitting mentioned in the passage?

4. What did another study suggest about the impact of standing for 3-4 hours a day over a year?

5. What do the experts recommend if people do use standing desks?

II. Translation

Directions: *Translate the following sentences from the text into Chinese.*

1. Whether it's working at a desk, sitting motionless in a car, bus or train or lounging on the sofa watching TV, we have a much more sedentary lifestyle than our parents and grandparents did.

2. It showed that drivers, who spent many hours sitting at the wheel, were twice as likely to have heart attacks than the more active ticket collectors.

3. In fact, sitting for a long time has been linked to a number of different health problems, even in people who otherwise exercise regularly.

4. One small study showed that office workers who stood for three hours after lunch had a much smaller increase in blood sugar levels.

5. They also point out that there are many alternatives to sitting, and that their impact is unlikely to be the same: walking, for example, burns far more calories than standing.

Unit 5 Work and Life

> 就业是最基本的民生。强化就业优先政策，健全就业促进机制，促进高质量充分就业。健全就业公共服务体系，完善重点群体就业支持体系，加强困难群体就业兜底帮扶。
>
> We need to intensify efforts to implement the employment-first policy and improve related mechanisms to promote high-quality and full employment. We will refine the public services system for employment and the system of providing employment support for key groups and do more to help those in difficulty find employment and meet their basic needs.
>
> 习近平《中国共产党第二十次全国代表大会报告》，2022年10月16日

Part One
Warming-up Questions

Directions: Read the following questions and share your answers with your classmates.

1. What skills do you think are essential for success in your field?
2. How do you handle stress and pressure in the workplace?
3. What role does teamwork play in your job?
4. How do you approach setting and achieving professional goals?
5. What challenges have you faced in your career, and how did you overcome them?

Useful Words and Expressions

resume 简历	interview 面试	manager 经理
promotion 晋升	commute 通勤	dedication 投入
initiative 主动性	leadership 领导力	responsibility 责任心
internship 实习	salary 工资	benefits 福利
performance 绩效	training 培训	feedback 反馈

Part Two
Text Studies

While many people follow traditional career paths, there are countless unique and unusual job opportunities waiting to be discovered across the globe. Let's read the following articles and find more information.

Text A

Interesting Jobs Around the World

Have you ever thought about doing a job that not many people have done before? There are many unique and **extraordinary** jobs around the world that **offer** different kinds of work experience and allow you to **explore** your **creativity**, skills, and interests in a way that is different from most other jobs. Here are five of them:

Ice Cream Taster in England

Do you love ice cream? If so, you could become an ice cream taster in England. This job **requires** tasting different flavors of ice cream and giving **feedback** on the **flavors** and **textures**. This helps companies create new recipes or improve existing ones. Ice cream tasters must be able to describe their tasting experiences clearly.

Penguin Keeper in Antarctica

Penguin keepers are responsible for caring for penguin colonies in the **harsh** Antarctic environment. They must have a strong interest in wildlife **conservation** and be willing to adapt to the **challenges** of living and working in this **remote** and difficult region. Penguin keepers **observe** the penguins' **behavior** and ensure their safety and well-being, which helps **preserve** the delicate Antarctic ecosystems.

Dialect Coach in the United Kingdom

In the world of acting, **dialect** coaches play a crucial role in helping actors master regional **accents** and speech patterns. This ensures that the characters they **portray** on stage or screen are **authentic**. Dialect coaches must have an in-depth understanding of the subtle differences in language and the ability to effectively teach these nuances to the actors.

Translator for Endangered Languages

For those who are **fascinated** by language **preservation**, the job of a translator for endangered languages offers a unique opportunity to make a lasting impact. These translators work to document and preserve languages that are at risk of disappearing, ensuring that the rich cultural **heritage** they represent is not lost. This role requires fluency in the endangered language, as well as a deep understanding of the historical and cultural contexts that have shaped it.

Professional Mourner in Japan

In Japan, there is a unique profession called "Professional Mourner". These individuals are hired to attend **funerals** and express grief and sorrow on behalf of the bereaved family. Professional mourners must have the emotional intelligence to convey genuine and heartfelt mourning, as well as the ability to adapt their performance to the **specific** cultural and religious traditions of the deceased. This role highlights the importance of honoring and preserving cultural rituals.

These five unique and **captivating** careers are just a small **glimpse** into the vast array of extraordinary job opportunities that exist around the world. By embracing **unconventional** paths, individuals can unlock a world of unique experiences, personal growth, and the opportunity to make a meaningful impact in their chosen fields.

New Words

extraordinary /ɪkˌstrɔː(r)dəneri/ *adj.*	非凡的，特别的
offer /ˈɒfə(r)/ *v.*	提供
explore /ɪkˈsplɔː(r)/ *v.*	探索
creativity /ˌkriːeɪˈtɪvɪti/ *n.*	创造力
require /rɪˈkwaɪə(r)/ *v.*	需要
feedback /ˈfiːdbak/ *n.*	反馈
flavor /ˈfleɪvə(r)/ *n.*	风味
texture /ˈtekstʃə(r)/ *n.*	质地
penguin /ˈpeŋgwɪn/ *n.*	企鹅
harsh /hɑː(r)ʃ/ *adj.*	严酷的
conservation /ˌkɒnsə(r)ˈveɪʃ(ə)n/ *n.*	保护
challenge /ˈtʃælɪndʒ/ *n.*	挑战
remote /rɪˈməʊt/ *adj.*	偏远的
observe /əbˈzɜː(r)v/ *v.*	观察
behavior /bɪˈheɪvjə(r)/ *n.*	行为
preserve /prɪˈzɜː(r)v/ *v.*	保护，保留
dialect /ˈdaɪəlekt/ *n.*	方言

accent /ˈæksent/ n.	口音
portray /pɔː(r)ˈtreɪ/ v.	描述，描绘
authentic /ɔːˈθentɪk/ adj.	真实的，正宗的
fascinate /ˈfæsɪneɪt/ v.	迷住，吸引
preservation /ˌprezə(r)ˈveɪʃ(ə)n/ n.	保护，维护
heritage /ˈherɪtɪdʒ/ n.	遗产
funeral /ˈfjuːnər(ə)l/ n.	葬礼
specific /spəˈsɪfɪk/ adj.	特定的
captivating /ˈkæptɪveɪtɪŋ/ adj.	迷人的
glimpse /glɪmps/ n.	一瞥
unconventional /ˌʌnkənˈvenʃ(ə)n(ə)l/ adj.	非传统的

Phrases and Expressions

be different from	与……不同
be responsible for	负责
have an interest in	对……有兴趣
be willing to	愿意，乐意
be fascinated by	被……所吸引
at risk of	面临……的风险
as well as	以及
on behalf of	代表
the vast array of	大量的，广泛的

Exercises

I. Understanding the text

Directions: *Answer the following questions according to the text.*

1. What is the job of an ice cream taster in England?
_____

2. Why is the role of a dialect coach important in the world of acting?
_____

3. What are the challenges that a penguin keeper in Antarctica must be willing to adapt to?
_____

4. How does the work of a translator for endangered languages contribute to language preserva-

tion?

5. What is the unique cultural significance of the role of a professional mourner in Japan?

Ⅱ. **Vocabulary and phrases**

Directions: *Fill in the blanks with the words given below. Change the form where necessary. Each word can be used only once.*

| feedback | offer | challenge | preserve | remote |
| harsh | require | observe | explore | specific |

1. This online course _____ flexible learning options to accommodate busy schedules.

2. Hiking in the mountains _____ proper equipment, physical fitness, and safety precautions.

3. The customer _____ on the product's features and performance is crucial for product development.

4. The _____ working environment in the factory led to high employee turnover and low productivity.

5. The company is facing a number of regulatory _____ that require a comprehensive compliance strategy.

6. The national park's mission is to _____ the natural habitats and protect endangered species.

7. How much do you _____ for this house?

8. The marketing campaign will target both online _____ offline channels to reach the target audience.

9. Each person has _____ needs when it comes to nutrition.

10. The children were excited to _____ the museum and learn about history.

Ⅲ. **Translation**

Directions: *Translate the following sentences into Chinese.*

1. This job requires tasting different flavors of ice cream and giving feedback on the flavors and textures.

2. They must have a strong interest in wildlife conservation and be willing to adapt to the challenges of living and working in this remote and difficult region.

3. For those who are fascinated by language preservation, the job of a translator for endangered languages offers a unique opportunity to make a lasting impact.

4. These individuals are hired to attend funerals and express grief and sorrow on behalf of the bereaved family.

5. These five unique and captivating careers are just a small glimpse into the vast array of extraordinary job opportunities that exist around the world.

Ⅳ. Writing

Directions: *An ideal job not only brings us financial stability, but also promotes our overall personal development and the realization of our self-worth. Why is career choice important for individual development? How should we choose a job that fits us? Please write an essay based on the above questions with no less than 100 words.*

Text B

The Life of a Professional Gamer

From the 1970s, video games have evolved a lot and become more immersive. But it's not just the graphics and gameplay mechanics that have changed. This evolution has also given rise to a new career path: that of the professional gamer.

In the early days of gaming, those passionate about video games often found themselves working behind the scenes as developers, testers, or coders. While competitive gaming events existed, they were largely viewed as hobbies rather than viable career options. However, the rise of live streaming platforms in the late 2000s paved the way for gamers to become celebrities.

Today, with e-sports now an integral part of gaming, what does a professional gamer's life look like? The key, according to many progamers, is practice, which is the same with many sports. While choosing the best equipment is important, such as the right controller or keyboard, most progamers spend hours every day working out hacks to save time or improve their chances of winning. And it's not just while playing games that they need to be active, but also in real life. Exercising and stretching is vital to avoid injuries to their backs and wrists and preventing eye fatigue from spending long hours staring at monitors by taking regular screen breaks.

But it's not just the physical aspects that gamers need to be careful with. According to some experts, like Dr Phil Birch, while the physical demands of e-sports and traditional sports are very different, the psychological impacts can be similar: regulating emotions, dealing with pressure and big crowds, and overcoming injury are just some of the common factors.

So, while the life of a professional gamer may appear glamorous and carefree, it is, in reality, a pursuit that demands unwavering dedication and discipline. The transition from amateur to pro is paved with countless hours of practice, perseverance, and the willingness to adapt to the unique demands of this rapidly growing industry.

Exercises

Ⅰ. **Understanding the text**.

Directions: *Answer the following questions according to the text.*

1. What new career path has the evolution of video games given rise to?

2. What do professional gamers spend hours every day doing?

3. Why is exercising and stretching vital for professional gamers?

4. What are the psychological impacts that professional gamers need to be careful with, according to experts?

5. What qualities are required for the transition from amateur to pro for professional gamers?

Ⅱ. **Translation**

Directions: *Translate the following sentences from the text into Chinese.*

1. In the early days of gaming, those passionate about video games often found themselves working behind the scenes as developers, testers, or coders.

2. While choosing the best equipment is important, such as the right controller or keyboard, most progamers spend hours every day working out hacks to save time or improve their chances of winning.

3. Regulating emotions, dealing with pressure and big crowds, and overcoming injury are just some of the common factors.

4. So, while the life of a professional gamer may appear glamorous and carefree, it is, in reality, a pursuit that demands unwavering dedication and discipline.

5. The transition from amateur to pro is paved with countless hours of practice, perseverance, and the willingness to adapt to the unique demands of this rapidly growing industry.

Unit 6 Starting a Business

> 完善促进创业带动就业的保障制度，支持和规范发展新就业形态。健全劳动法律法规，完善劳动关系协商协调机制，完善劳动者权益保障制度，加强灵活就业和新就业形态劳动者权益保障。
>
> We will improve the system for creating jobs by encouraging business startups and support and regulate the development of new forms of employment. We will improve labor laws and regulations, the mechanisms for labor relation consultations and mediation, and the systems for safeguarding workers' rights and interests, and we will do more to protect the rights and interests of those in flexible employment and new forms of employment.
>
> 习近平《中国共产党第二十次全国代表大会报告》，2022年10月16日

Part One
Warming-up Questions

Directions: *Read the following questions and share your answers with your classmates.*

1. What are some of the key challenges that entrepreneurs typically face when starting a new business?

2. In what ways can entrepreneurs make use of social media to grow their new business?

3. What are some of the key factors we would consider when deciding whether to start our own business?

4. What are the main advantages of being your own boss as an entrepreneur?

Useful Words and Expressions

entrepreneur 企业家	investment 投资	revenue 收入
expense 支出	marketing 营销	promotion 推广
operation 运营	human resources 人力资源	leadership 领导力
resilience 韧性	social impact 社会影响力	passion 激情

Part Two
Text Studies

Nowadays, it can be seen that young entrepreneurs starting up businesses all over the world. Even people who already have regular jobs are often running side projects as well. How can you become successful in your career? And how can you keep yourself feeling happy and fulfilled in your work? Let's take a close look at the following articles below—maybe we can pick up some useful insights.

Text A

Young People in Business

Do you have a business brain? Are you always looking for the next big idea? Maybe, like me, you might feel setting up a new company is something you might do when you're older, when you have more experience. But that's not always the case.

While some of us may feel young **adulthood** is a time of **tentatively** finding our place in the world, sleeping late and partying hard, others are already on a path to great business **success**. Take the founder of Microsoft, Bill Gates, who started his company as a young **university** student at Harvard in the US. There are many other examples of young entrepreneurs who have become hugely successful, proving that there's no minimum age to becoming top dog.

But to be the next business **executive** requires effort. You need to develop a sharp **intellect** and strong business skills. But most importantly, you must have **enthusiasm** and passion for your work. Starting a new business comes with an element of risk but if you are able to **spot** the next big idea, it's probably worth giving it a try. Jessica Rose owns a **jewellery** making business and **admits** that "when I first started I had no business training whatsoever…but I kind of woke up one day and thought I'd really love to be a jewellery designer." She went on to be a successful young entrepreneur.

Being young and in business does have its **drawbacks**; you may worry you have nothing to bring to the table and that the people who work for you tend to be older and wiser. That's what young British entrepreneur Sacranie found. He started his third business while studying **chemistry** at university. He says "now I've got two additional directors who have **grey** hair" but when they first started he says he "could tell they were thinking in the back of their heads, 'I've got a kid sitting in front of me.'"

You may think setting up a new **start-up** is easier said than done. As well as ideas, you need **financial** backing and expert guidance. But if you're studying hard at university and don't have the **desire** to go into business and make your fortune, keep on studying—an education is **priceless**!

New Words

adulthood /ˈædəlthʊd/ n.　　　　成年，成年期，成熟
tentatively /ˈtɛntətɪvli/ adv.　　　暂时性地，试探性地
success /səkˈsɛs/ n.　　　　　　成功
university /ˌjuːnɪˈvɜːrsɪti/ n.　　　大学
prove /pruːv/ v.　　　　　　　证明，表明
minimum /ˈmɪnɪməm/ adj.　　　最小的，最低的

executive /ɪgˈzɛkjətɪv/	n.	高级管理人员
intellect /ˈɪntəlɛkt/	n.	智力，智慧
enthusiasm /ɪnˈθjuːziæzəm/	n.	热情
spot /spɒt/	v.	发现
jewellery /ˈdʒuːəlri/	n.	珠宝
admit /ədˈmɪt/	v.	承认
drawback /ˈdrɔːbæk/	n.	缺点
chemistry /ˈkɛmɪstri/	n.	化学
grey /greɪ/	adj.	灰色的
start-up /ˈstɑːtʌp/	n.	初创企业
financial /faɪˈnænʃəl/	adj.	金融的，财务的
desire /dɪˈzaɪər/	n.	欲望，渴望
priceless /ˈpraɪsləs/	adj.	无价的

Phrases and Expressions

set up	建立，设立
on a path to	通往，走向
be worth doing	值得做
give it a try	试一试
wake up	醒来
tend to	往往，常常
in front of	在……前面
make one's fortune	发财，致富

Cultural Notes

entrepreneur	企业家，是指自己创立并运营企业的人。企业家具有创新精神和冒险精神，能够组建和管理团队，协调各种资源实现商业目标

Exercises

Ⅰ. Understanding the text

Directions: *Answer the following questions according to the text.*

1. What does the passage suggest about the mindset of some young adults when it comes to star-

ting a business?

___

2. What is the most important quality an entrepreneur needs?

___

3. What drawback that young entrepreneurs may face?

___

4. What is required to start a new business besides just ideas?

___

5. According to the passage, what is the key advice given for those who do not have a strong desire to go into business?

___

Ⅱ. **Vocabulary and phrases**

Directions: *Fill in the blanks with the words given below. Change the form where necessary. Each word can be used only once.*

| desire | prove | minimum | spot | admit |
| intellect | executive | priceless | enthusiasm | drawback |

1. The company has set a _____ order quantity of 500 units to ensure profitability.

2. While hiking, I _____ a rare bird resting on a tree branch.

3. Her _____ to travel the world motivated her to save money.

4. The memories we create with our loved ones are truly _____ and cannot be measured in money.

5. The company's advertising is _____ their product is the most eco-friendly.

6. The CEO _____ that the company had made some mistakes in its financial reporting.

7. One major _____ of working from home is the potential for distractions and lack of structure.

8. She was promoted to an _____ position after years of hard work.

9. She expressed her _____ for learning new languages.

10. Applying your _____ to innovative work can lead to breakthroughs.

Ⅲ. **Translation**

Directions: *Translate the following sentences into Chinese.*

1. There are many other examples of young entrepreneurs who have become hugely successful, proving that there's no minimum age to becoming top dog.

___

2. You need to develop a sharp intellect and strong business skills.
_____

3. Being young and in business does have its drawbacks; you may worry you have nothing to bring to the table and that the people who work for you tend to be older and wiser.
_____

4. You may think setting up a new start-up is easier said than done.
_____

5. As well as ideas, you need financial backing and expert guidance.
_____

Ⅳ. Writing

Directions: Write an essay that begins with the sentence "Nowadays more and more people choose to start their own business." You can make comments, use examples, or use your personal experiences to develop your essay. You should write at least 100 words.

Text B

Side Hustles

Do you have a job? If you do, you'll know the world of work can be tough—long hours, tedious tasks and stress. But it can bring benefits too, such as a regular salary and, sometimes, job satisfaction. Maybe that's why more and more people are now taking on a side hustle—another name for a second job.

For some having two jobs is a necessity—a way to make ends meet and provide extra income. But it now seems that more people want to put their skills and passions into practice to make money. These tend to be entrepreneurial young people who want to work on their own projects alongside their main source of income.

According to Henley Business School, around one in four workers run at least one side hustle business, half of which were started in the past two years. Those aged 25 to 34 are most likely to be involved, with 37% thought to run a sideline of some kind. It calculates that the average side hustler makes about 20% of their income through their second job.

But what's interesting is that many millennials (千禧一代) are turning their hand to new jobs not just for money and security. Research has found that almost three-quarters of people are following a passion or exploring a new challenge. Zhou Xiaobai works some of the time for a telecommunications company to pay the bills, but spends the rest of her time developing her crafting company. She says going full-time is "not financially worth it right now but it fuels my creative soul and makes me happy".

Mobile apps have also aided the more commercially minded side hustler. Peer-to-peer firms such as Meituan, Xianyu, Pinduoduo and Zhihu, allow users to do everything from odd jobs to renting out homes and parking spaces from their mobile phone.

Of course having a side hustle means you are self-employed—or freelance—which can give you flexibility to work when you like, but it can be risky. You sometime work on a zero-hours contract and may not get offered enough work. Or what was originally your passion may become more of a chore. However, this could be the best way to try out a new career or follow a passion while not giving up the day job.

Exercises

Ⅰ. Understanding the text.

Directions: *Answer the following questions according to the text.*

1. What is a side hustle?

2. On average, how much of their income do side hustlers make from their second job?

3. What are the reasons why millennials are turning to side hustles?

4. How have mobile apps aided the growth of side hustles?

5. How can a side hustle be beneficial for trying out a new career?

Ⅱ. Translation

Directions: *Translate the following sentences from the text into Chinese.*

1. But it can bring benefits too, such as a regular salary and, sometimes, job satisfaction.

2. For some having two jobs is a necessity—a way to make ends meet and provide extra income.

3. These tend to be entrepreneurial young people who want to work on their own projects alongside their main source of income.

4. Mobile apps have also aided the more commercially minded side hustler.

5. Of course having a side hustle means you are self-employed—or freelance—which can give you flexibility to work when you like, but it can be risky.

Unit 7　Leisure Activities

> 中国式现代化是物质文明和精神文明相协调的现代化。物质富足、精神富有是社会主义现代化的根本要求。物质贫困不是社会主义，精神贫乏也不是社会主义。我们不断厚植现代化的物质基础，不断夯实人民幸福生活的物质条件，同时大力发展社会主义先进文化，加强理想信念教育，传承中华文明，促进物的全面丰富和人的全面发展。
>
> It is the modernization of material and cultural-ethical advancement. Material abundance and cultural-ethical enrichment are fundamental goals of socialist modernization. Material want is not socialism, nor is cultural impoverishment. While continuing to consolidate the material foundation for modernization and improve the material conditions for people's wellbeing, we will strive to develop advanced socialist culture, foster strong ideals and convictions, and carry forward China's cultural heritage. We will thus promote all-around material abundance as well as people's well-rounded development.
>
> 习近平《中国共产党第二十次全国代表大会报告》，2022 年 10 月 16 日

Part One
Warming-up Questions

Directions: *Read the following questions and share your answers with your classmates.*

1. What recreational activities do you most enjoy participating in during your leisure time?

2. Can you describe any hobbies or interests you have been pursuing recently?

3. In your opinion, what are the key benefits that leisure activities can provide?

4. What role does technology play in your leisure time activities?

5. Describe a traditional Chinese sport or leisure activity in English, such as martial arts, Jianzi (shuttlecock kicking), Chinese chess, or bamboo pole dance.

Useful Words and Expressions

recreation 娱乐、休闲	hobby 爱好、嗜好	leisure 闲暇时间、休闲
relaxation 放松、休息	entertainment 娱乐、消遣	outdoor 户外的
socialize 社交、交际	travel 旅行、游历	reading 阅读
gardening 园艺、种植	meditation 冥想	culinary 烹饪的

Part Two
Text Studies

People in today's society enjoy a wide range of leisure activities, from adventurous outdoor pursuits to relaxing hobbies, catering to their diverse interests and lifestyles. Let's read the following articles to find more information.

Text A

Why Camping can be so Much Fun?

When you go on holiday, where do you like to stay? Do you like the luxury of a **five-star** hotel, the convenience of a **self-catering** apartment or do you prefer the freedom of sleeping under canvas? If you haven't tried the latter, maybe you should join the increasing number of people who are enjoying the simple pleasures of **camping**.

By grabbing your **tent**, and some additional **accessories**, it's easy to head off to the countryside and enjoy a night or two under the stars. Many **campers** are **ditching** the trappings of their modern, **hectic** life to do this, encouraged by experts who say a few peaceful nights in the middle of nowhere might be a good way to unwind and improve our sleep patterns and well-being. It is also, of course, a good **low-budget** holiday option. For the **adventurous**, wild camping is the ultimate escape from reality. Armed with just some food and a sleeping bag, you're free from rules, away from other people, and able to enjoy the **back-to-basics** experience. One wild camper, Phoebe Smith, stated: "The act of sleeping when everybody else has gone home—when you **notice** the wildlife and the stars—is one of the best things in life."

But for those who still want some home comforts, a **campsite** is a more suitable place to **pitch** your tent. Here you have **facilities** such as washrooms, a shop and maybe even a restaurant. And for the most **luxurious** camping experience, you could try **glamping**. In the UK, camping—and **caravanning**—has always been popular. One survey by Visit Britain found around 4.38 million people go camping in Britain every year.

More recently, sales of camping gear have jumped as more people have opted for a **staycation** within the UK. One camping retailer, Halfords, reported a surge in demand for products such as stoves, cool boxes and camping chairs. With the addition of **inflatable mattresses** and **pillows**, powerful **torches** and lamps to light up your tent and a better selection of **easy-to-cook** food, you can almost **guarantee** a comfortable and enjoyable camping expedition. The only thing you can't guarantee, in the UK at least, is good weather!

New Words

five-star /ˌfaɪvˈstɑr/ *adj.*	五星级的
self-catering /ˌsɛlfˈkeɪtərɪŋ/ *adj.*	自助式的
camping /ˈkæmpɪŋ/ *n.*	露营
tent /tɛnt/ *n.*	帐篷
accessory /əkˈsɛsəri/ *n.*	配件

camper /ˈkæmpər/ n.	露营者
ditch /dɪtʃ/ v.	抛弃，丢弃
hectic /ˈhɛktɪk/ adj.	忙碌的
low-budget /ˌloʊˈbʌdʒɪt/ adj.	低预算的
adventurous /ədˈvɛntʃərəs/ adj.	有冒险精神的
back-to-basics /ˌbæktəˈbæsɪks/ adj.	回归本真的
notice /ˈnoʊtɪs/ v.	注意到，发现
campsite /ˈkæmpsaɪt/ n.	露营地
pitch /pɪtʃ/ v.	搭建（帐篷）
facility /fəˈsɪləti/ n.	设施
luxurious /lʌgˈʒʊriəs/ adj.	豪华的
glamping /ˈglæmpɪŋ/ n.	豪华露营
caravanning /ˈkærəvænɪŋ/ n.	露营车旅行
staycation /ˈsteɪkeɪʃən/ n.	在家度假
stove /stoʊv/ n.	炉灶
inflatable /ɪnˈfleɪtəbəl/ adj.	充气的
mattress /ˈmætrɪs/ n.	床垫
pillow /ˈpɪloʊ/ n.	枕头
torch /tɔrtʃ/ n.	手电筒
easy-to-cook /ˌizi tə ˈkʊk/ adj.	易煮的
guarantee /ˌgærənˈtiː/ v.	保证

Phrases and Expressions

under canvas	在帐篷下
head off	出发，前往
under the stars	在星空下
in the middle of nowhere	在偏远的地方，在茫茫荒野中
wild camping	野外露营
sleeping bag	睡袋
home comforts	家庭式舒适

opt for 选择

light up 照亮

Cultural Notes

staycation/ˈsteɪkeɪʃən/ n.	在家度假。Staycation 是由两个词组合而成的："stay"（停留）和 "vacation"（假期）。是指在本地或家附近度假的一种方式，通常不需要长途旅行。人们在假期期间选择留在自己的城市，享受当地的景点、餐馆和活动，而不是去外地旅行

Exercises

Ⅰ. Understanding the text

Directions：*Answer the following questions according to the text.*

1. What are the three options for accommodation when going on holiday, according to the passage?
_____

2. What does the passage say about the experts' advice on camping?
_____

3. What has caused a surge in demand for camping gear?
_____

4. What additional items can help guarantee a comfortable and enjoyable camping expedition?
_____

5. What does the "back-to-basics experience" of wild camping involves?
_____

Ⅱ. Vocabulary and phrases

Directions：*Fill in the blanks with the words given below. Change the form where necessary. Each word can be used only once.*

facility	adventure	accessory	notification	budget
hectic	luxurious	guarantee	cater	opt

1. The new sports _____ includes a gym, swimming pool, and tennis courts.

2. Sunglasses are an essential _____ for protecting your eyes from the sun's harmful UV rays.

3. My schedule has been quite _____ this week with back-to-back meetings.

4. She has an _____ spirit and loves trying new activities like rock climbing.

5. I received a _____ on my phone about the upcoming meeting.

6. We need to create a _____ to manage our monthly expenses effectively.

7. Five-star resorts are known for their _____ accommodations and personalized service.

8. After much consideration, the committee _____ for the proposal that included the new initiative.

9. The warranty will _____ the appliance for five years.

10. She decided to _____ for the party herself to ensure everything was exactly as she wanted.

Ⅲ. Translation

Directions: *Translate the following sentences into Chinese.*

1. By grabbing your tent, and some additional accessories, it's easy to head off to the countryside and enjoy a night or two under the stars.

_____

2. Many campers are ditching the trappings of their modern, hectic life to do this, encouraged by experts who say a few peaceful nights in the middle of nowhere might be a good way to unwind and improve our sleep patterns and well-being.

_____

3. For the adventurous, wild camping is the ultimate escape from reality.

_____

4. Armed with just some food and a sleeping bag, you're free from rules, away from other people, and able to enjoy the back-to-basics experience.

_____

5. More recently, sales of camping gear have jumped as more people have opted for a staycation within the UK.

_____

Ⅳ. Writing

Directions: Write a short essay on relaxation methods. Your essay should include the benefits of various relaxation methods and the importance of developing good relaxation habits. You are required to write at least 100 words.

Text B

The Benefits of Singing

Whether you're a karaoke superstar or simply enjoy singing in the privacy of your own shower, research shows that singing can provide both physical and mental health benefits. And you don't even have to be good at it!

The physical and mental advantages of singing are caused by a combination of factors, according to Baishali Mukherjee from the World Federation of Music Therapy. Mukherjee explained that the physical effort required in singing—such as taking deep breaths, controlling the vocal cords, and moving the mouth and body—is one reason why it can elevate mood. Precisely hitting each note involves breathing control and the use of the diaphragm. This can lead to an increase of oxygen intake and lung capacity.

Also, apparently, singing in a group brings just as many benefits as singing solo. It has been estimated that over 2.2 million people in Britain now regularly sing in a choir. A choir can be amateur or professional and is made up of people who sing together, often in harmony with different people singing different parts, such as soprano or tenor, according to their vocal range.

A 2022 University of Vienna study found that choral singing enhances feelings of trust and bonding among a group, which can help with depression and loneliness. And, aside from mood-boosting, other proven mental health benefits of singing include a lowering of stress and anxiety levels due to the release of endorphins—the so-called "happy hormones".

So, whether you are a confident singer or not, give singing a go! You don't need an instrument because that's you. Yes, you may occasionally forget the lyrics or sound a bit off-key, but remember that the benefits of singing are plentiful.

Exercises

Ⅰ. **Understanding the text**.

Directions: *Answer the following questions according to the text.*

1. What factors contribute to the physical and mental health benefits of singing according to the article?

2. How can singing lead to an increase in oxygen intake and lung capacity?

3. The article mentions that over 2.2 million people in Britain now regularly sing in a choir. What is the significance of this statistic?

4. According to the University of Vienna study, what are the benefits of choral singing?

5. Even if someone is not a confident singer, should they still try singing? Why?

Ⅱ. **Translation**

Directions: *Translate the following sentences from the text into Chinese.*

1. Whether you're a karaoke superstar or simply enjoy singing in the privacy of your own shower, research shows that singing can provide both physical and mental health benefits.

2. Precisely hitting each note involves breathing control and the use of the diaphragm. This can lead to an increase of oxygen intake and lung capacity.

3. It has been estimated that over 2.2 million people in Britain now regularly sing in a choir.

4. Choral singing enhances feelings of trust and bonding among a group, which can help with depression and loneliness.

5. Yes, you may occasionally forget the lyrics or sound a bit off-key, but remember that the benefits of singing are plentiful.

Unit 8　Humor and Happiness

中华优秀传统文化源远流长、博大精深，是中华文明的智慧结晶，其中蕴含的天下为公、民为邦本、为政以德、革故鼎新、任人唯贤、天人合一、自强不息、厚德载物、讲信修睦、亲仁善邻等，是中国人民在长期生产生活中积累的宇宙观、天下观、社会观、道德观的重要体现，同科学社会主义价值观主张具有高度契合性。

With a history stretching back to antiquity, China's fine traditional culture is extensive and profound; it is the crystallization of the wisdom of Chinese civilization. Our traditional culture espouses many important principles and concepts, including pursuing common good for all; regarding the people as the foundation of the state; governing by virtue; discarding the outdated in favor of the new; selecting officials on the basis of merit; promoting harmony between humanity and nature; ceaselessly pursuing self-improvement; embracing the world with virtue; acting in good faith and being friendly to others; and fostering neighborliness. These maxims, which have taken shape over centuries of work and life, reflect the Chinese people's way of viewing the universe, the world, society, and morality and are highly consistent with the values and propositions of scientific socialism.

习近平《中国共产党第二十次全国代表大会报告》，2022年10月16日

Part One
Warming-up Questions

Directions: *Read the following questions and share your answers with your classmates.*

1. In what ways can humor reduce stress and create a more relaxed environment?

2. Does humor help facilitate interaction and improve relationships?

3. What problems can arise from overusing humor? How can a balanced approach be maintained?

4. Can humor boost self-confidence and positive attitudes? How?

5. How can we develop a sense of humor?

Useful Words and Expressions

laughter 笑声	joke 笑话	comedy 喜剧
amusing 引人发笑的	pun 双关语	quip 俏皮话
drollery 古怪幽默	funny 有趣的，好笑的	wit 智慧，机智
parody 仿拟，戏仿	punchline 笑点	guffaw 狂笑

Part Two

Text Studies

Humor is a very powerful thing. When we laugh, our brain releases a chemical called endorphins, which instantly puts us in a good mood. Humor not only helps us relax and relieve stress, but it can also boost our immune system and even lower our blood pressure. Let's learn more about the power of humor by reading the following articles.

Text A

The Power of Laughter

Laughter is strong **medicine**. This simple act can draw people together in ways that **trigger** healthy physical and emotional changes in the body. Laughter strengthens the **immune** system, boosts mood, **diminishes** pain, and protects against the damaging effects of stress. Nothing works faster or more **dependably** to bring the mind and body back into balance than a good laugh.

Humor lightens **burdens**, **inspires** hope, connects people to one another, and keeps us focused and **alert**. It also helps release anger and **facilitate** forgiveness. With so much power to heal and renew, the ability to laugh easily and frequently is a **resource** for solving problems, enhancing relationships, and supporting both physical and emotional health. This priceless medicine is fun, free, and easy to use.

Laughter offers a wide range of powerful benefits. It relaxes the body by relieving **tension** and stress, leaving muscles relaxed for up to 45 minutes. Laughter also boosts the immune system by decreasing stress **hormones** and increasing **infection-fighting** antibodies. While not a **replacement** for exercise, laughter can modestly burn calories as well. Furthermore, laughter **diffuses** anger and conflict, and some research suggests it may even increase **longevity**. **Incorporating** more laughter into our daily lives can be a simple yet highly effective way to improve our overall physical and mental state.

As children, we used to laugh hundreds of times a day, but as adults, life tends to be more serious and laughter more **infrequent**. By intentionally seeking out more opportunities for humor and laughter, however, we can improve our emotional health, strengthen our relationships, find greater happiness—and potentially even add years to our lives.

An essential **ingredient** for developing our sense of humor is learning not to take ourselves too seriously and laugh at our own mistakes. While some events in life are clearly sad, most do not carry an overwhelming sense of either sadness or delight. So, let's choose to laugh whenever we can.

The ability to laugh, play, and have fun not only makes life more enjoyable, but also helps us solve problems, connect with others, and think more creatively. People who find humor in their daily lives find that it renews them and all of their relationships. With humor, we can often transform a problem into an opportunity for creative learning.

New Words

medicine /ˈmedɪsɪn/ n.	药物，医学
trigger /ˈtrɪgər/ v.	触发，引发
immune /ɪˈmjuːn/ adj.	免疫的
diminish /dɪˈmɪnɪʃ/ v.	减少，降低
dependably /dɪˈpendəbli/ adv.	可靠地
burden /ˈbɜːdən/ n.	负担
inspire /ɪnˈspaɪər/ v.	鼓舞，激发
alert /əˈlɜːrt/ adj.	警惕的
facilitate /fəˈsɪlɪteɪt/ v.	促进，实现
tension /ˈtenʃən/ n.	紧张
hormone /ˈhɔːmoʊn/ n.	激素
infection-fighting /ɪnˈfekʃənˈfaɪtɪŋ/ adj.	抗感染的
replacement /rɪˈpleɪsmənt/ n.	替代品
modestly /ˈmɒdɪstli/ adv.	谦逊地
diffuse /dɪˈfjuːz/ v.	散布，使分散
longevity /lɒnˈdʒevɪti/ n.	长寿
incorporate /ɪnˈkɔːpəreɪt/ v.	融入，吸收
infrequent /ɪnˈfriːkwənt/ adj.	不频繁的
ingredient /ɪnˈgriːdiənt/ n.	成分

Phrases and Expressions

bring…back into…	让……恢复……
a wide range of	广泛的，多种多样的
hundreds of	成百上千
seek out	寻找……探索……
laugh at	嘲笑……
not only…but also…	不仅……而且……
connect with	与……建立联系
transform…into…	把……转变为……

Cultural Notes

the immune system	免疫系统，是人体重要的防御系统，主要包括细胞免疫和体液免疫。免疫系统是人体防御机制的核心，能够识别并清除各种病原体和有害物质，维持机体内部环境的稳定

Exercises

Ⅰ. Understanding the text.

Directions：*Answer the following questions according to the text.*

1. What are the benefits of laughter according to the passage?

_____

2. What does the passage say about the ability to laugh easily and frequently as a resource?

_____

3. What does the frequency of laughter between children and adults?

_____

4. What is an essential ingredient for developing a sense of humor?

_____

5. What is the connection between laughter and creative thinking?

_____

Ⅱ. Vocabulary and phrases

Directions：*Fill in the blanks with the words given below. Change the form where necessary. Each word can be used only once.*

| trigger | diminish | burden | inspire | alert |
| tension | diffuse | immune | ingredient | range |

1. The clouds in the sky slowly _____ as the sun started to shine brighter.

2. Reading biographies of successful entrepreneurs can _____ individuals to start their own businesses.

3. The announcement of the new policy _____ a heated debate among employees.

4. Vaccination helps make individuals _____ to specific diseases.

5. The heavy workload and long hours have become a significant _____ for the employees.

6. Fresh parsley（香菜）are a key _____ in making a flavorful pesto sauce.

7. Engaging in open communication can _____ conflicts and misunderstandings.

8. The store offers a wide _____ of products, from electronics to clothing.

9. Practicing deep breathing can help relieve the _____ in your body.

10. The _____ security guard noticed the suspicious activity and immediately called the police.

Ⅲ. Translation

Directions: *Translate the following sentences from the text into Chinese.*

1. Laughter strengthens the immune system, boosts mood, diminishes pain, and protects against the damaging effects of stress.

_____

2. Nothing works faster or more dependably to bring the mind and body back into balance than a good laugh.

_____

3. It relaxes the body by relieving tension and stress, leaving muscles relaxed for up to 45 minutes.

_____

4. Incorporating more laughter into our daily lives can be a simple yet highly effective way to improve our overall physical and mental state.

_____

5. While some events in life are clearly sad, most do not carry an overwhelming sense of either sadness or delight.

_____

Ⅳ. **Writing**

Directions: *In daily life, we inevitably encounter some embarrassing yet interesting things. Which one left the deepest impression on you? Did this happen to you or to someone else? How did it happen? Please write a composition of at least* 100 *words based on the above questions.*

Text B

The Bed Problem

Jack went to see a doctor. He had a big problem.

"Doctor," said Jack, "every time I lie in bed, I think there's someone under it. Then I get under the bed, and I think there's someone on top of it. It's driving me crazy!"

The doctor said, "Bring yourself to me three times a week for two years, and I'll cure your fears."

"How much do you charge?" Jack asked.

"A hundred dollars each visit." the doctor replied.

Jack thought about it. "I'll think about it." he said.

Six months went by, and the doctor saw Jack on the street.

"Why didn't you ever come see me again?" the doctor asked.

"For a hundred bucks a visit? No way!" said Jack. "I got cured for just 10 dollars."

"Is that so? How?" the doctor wanted to know.

"A carpenter fixed it for me," Jack explained. "He just told me to cut the legs off the bed!"

The simple solution the carpenter provided had cured Jack's problem for just a tiny fraction of what the doctor had wanted to charge. Jack had found a much more affordable way to fix his bed bug issue.

The doctor shook his head, realizing he had missed out on an easy way to help his patient. Jack had found a clever solution that worked for him, without having to pay the high medical fees.

Sometimes the simplest answer is the best. Jack's carpenter friend had listened to the problem and come up with an ingenious, cost-effective fix. The doctor, on the other hand, had been too focused on a long, expensive treatment plan.

In the end, Jack got the help he needed for just 10 dollars, while the doctor missed out on a potentially lucrative patient. It just goes to show that the most practical solution isn't always the most obvious one.

Exercises

Ⅰ. **Understanding the text**.

Directions: *Read the above text carefully and choose the best answer to each question.*

1. What was Jack's main problem when he visited the doctor?

A) He couldn't sleep at night.

B) He thought there was someone under his bed.

C) He had a fear of heights.

D) He had a headache.

2. How much did the doctor charge per visit?

A) Ten dollars.

B) Fifty dollars.

C) One hundred dollars.

D) Two hundred dollars.

3. What alternative solution did Jack find to his problem?

A) He decided to sleep in a different room.

B) A carpenter suggested cutting the legs off the bed.

C) He bought a new bed.

D) He moved to another city.

4. Why did Jack choose not to continue seeing the doctor?

A) He didn't believe the doctor could help him.

B) He found the doctor's fees too expensive.

C) He moved to a different city.

D) He got better on his own.

5. What lesson can be learned from Jack's experience with the carpenter and the doctor?

A) Medical professionals always provide the best solutions.

B) Sometimes the simplest solution is the most effective.

C) Expensive treatments are necessary for serious problems.

D) It's better to avoid doctors entirely.

Ⅱ. **Translation**

Directions: *Translate the following sentences from the text into Chinese.*

1. Bring yourself to me three times a week for two years, and I'll cure your fears.

2. The simple solution the carpenter provided had cured Jack's problem for just a tiny fraction of what the doctor had wanted to charge.

3. Jack had found a clever solution that worked for him, without having to pay the high medical fees.

4. Jack's carpenter friend had listened to the problem and come up with an ingenious, cost-effective fix.

5. In the end, Jack got the help he needed for just 10 dollars, while the doctor missed out on a potentially lucrative patient.

第三部分 模拟试题

Model Test 1

Part One: Reading Comprehension (40%, 2 points each)

Direction: *There are 4 passages in this part. Each passage is followed by some questions or unfinished statements. For each of them there are four choices marked A, B, C and D. You should decide on the best choice and write the corresponding letter on **Answer Sheet**.*

Passage One
Questions 1 to 5 are based on the following passage.

By almost any measure, there is a boom in Internet-based instruction. In just a few years, 34 percent of American universities have begun offering some form of distance learning (DL), and among the larger school, it's closer to 90 percent. If you doubt the popularity of the trend, you probably haven't. It enrolls 90,000 student, a statistic used to support its claim to be the largest private university in the country.

While the kinds of instruction offered in these programs will differ, DL usually signifies a course in which the instructions post syllabi (课程大纲), reading assignments, and schedules on Websites, and students send in their assignments by e-mail. Generally speaking, face-to-face communication with an instructor is minimized or eliminated altogether.

The attraction for students might at first seem obvious. Primarily, there's the convenience promised by courses on the Net: you can do the work, as they say, in your pajamas (睡衣). But figures indicate that the reduced effort results in a reduced commitment to the course. While dropout rates for all freshmen at American universities is around 20 percent, the rate for online students is 35 percent. Students themselves seem to understand the weaknesses inherent in the setup. In a survey conducted for eCornell, the DL division of Cornell University, less than a third of the respondents expected the quality of the online course to be as good as the classroom course.

Clearly from the schools perspective, there's a lot of money to be saved. Although some of the more ambitious programs require new investments in servers and networks to support collaborative software, most DL courses can run on existing or minimally upgraded (升级) systems. The more students who enroll in a course but don't come to campus, the more the school saves on keeping the lights on in the classrooms, paying doorkeepers, and maintaining parking lots. And there's evidence that instructors must work harder to run a DL course for a variety of reasons, won't be paid any more, and might well be paid less.

1. What is the most striking feature of the University of Phoenix?

A) All its courses are offered online.

B) Its online courses are of the best quality.

C) It boasts the largest number of students on campus.

D) Anyone taking its online courses is sure to get a degree.

2. According to the passage, distance learning is basically characterized by _____.

A) a considerable flexibility in its academic requirements

B) the great diversity of students' academic backgrounds

C) a minimum or total absence of face-to-face instruction

D) the casual relationship between students and professors

3. Many students take Internet-based courses mainly because they can _____.

A) earn their academic degrees with much less effort

B) save a great deal on traveling and boarding expenses

C) select courses from various colleges and universities

D) work on the required courses whenever and wherever

4. What accounts for the high drop-out rates for online students?

A) There is no strict control over the academic standards of the courses.

B) The evaluation system used by online universities is inherently weak.

C) There is no mechanism to ensure that they make the required effort.

D) Lack of classroom interaction reduces the effectiveness of instruction.

5. According to the passage, universities show great enthusiasm for DL programs for the purpose of _____.

A) building up their reputation

B) cutting down on their expenses

C) upgrading their teaching facilities

D) providing convenience for students

Passage Two

Questions 6 to 10 are based on the following passage.

High-quality customer service is preached (宣扬) by many, but actually keeping customers happy is easier said than done.

Shoppers seldom complain to the manager or owner of a retail store, but instead will alert their friends, relatives, co-workers, strangers-and anyone who will listen.

Store managers are often the last to hear complaints, and often find out only when their regular customers decide to frequent their competitors, according to a study jointly conducted by Verde group and Wharton school

"Storytelling hurts retailers and entertains consumers," said Paula Courtney, President of the Verde group. "the store loses the customer, but the shopper must also find a replacement."

On average, every unhappy customer will complain to at least four other, and will no longer visit the specific store for every dissatisfied customer, a store will lose up to three more due to negative reviews. The resulting "snowball effect" can be disastrous to retailers.

According to the research, shoppers who purchased clothing encountered the most problems. ranked second and third were grocery and electronics customers.

The most common complaints include filled parking lots, cluttered (塞满了的) shelves, overloaded racks, out-of-stock items, long check-out lines, and rude salespeople.

During peak shopping hours, some retailers solved the parking problems by getting moonlighting (业余兼职的) local police to work as parking attendants. Some hired flag wavers to direct customers to empty parking spaces. This guidance eliminated the need for customers to circle the parking lot endlessly, and avoided confrontation between those eyeing the same parking space.

Retailers can relieve the headaches by redesigning store layouts, pre-stocking sales items, hiring speedy and experienced cashiers, and having sales representatives on hand to answer questions.

Most importantly, salespeople should be diplomatic and polite with angry customers.

"Retailers who're responsive and friendly are more likely to smooth over issues than those who aren't so friendly." said Professor Stephen Hoch. "Maybe something as simple as a greeter at the store entrance would help."

Customers can also improve future shopping experiences by filing complaints to the retailer, instead of complaining to the rest of the world. Retailers are hard-pressed to improve when they have no idea what is wrong.

6. Why are store managers often the last to hear complaints?

A) Most customers won't bother to complain even if they have had unhappy experiences.

B) Customers would rather relate their unhappy experiences to people around them.

C) Few customers believe the service will be improved.

D) Customers have no easy access to store managers.

7. What does Paula Courtney imply by saying "…the shopper must also find a replacement" (Para. 4)?

A) New customers are bound to replace old ones.

B) It is not likely the shopper can find the same products in other stores.

C) Most stores provide the same.

D) Not complaining to the manager causes the shopper some trouble too.

8. Shop owners often hire moonlighting police as parking attendants so that shoppers _____.

A) can stay longer browsing in the store

B) won't have trouble parking their cars

C) won't have any worries about security

D) can find their cars easily after shopping

9. What contributes most to smoothing over issues with customers?

A) Manners of the salespeople.

B) Hiring of efficient employees.

C) Huge supply of goods for sale.

D) Design of the store layout.

10. To achieve better shopping experiences, customers are advised to _____.

A) exert pressure on stores to improve their service

B) settle their disputes with stores in a diplomatic way

C) voice their dissatisfaction to store managers directly

D) shop around and make comparisons between stores

Passage Three

Questions 11 to 15 are based on the following passage.

You never see him, but they're with you every time you fly. They record where you are going, how fast you're traveling and whether everything on your airplane is functioning normally. Their ability to withstand almost any disaster makes them seem like something out of a comic book. They're known as the black box.

When planes fall from the sky, as a Yemeni airliner did on its way to Comoros Islands in the India ocean June 30, 2009, the black box is the best bet for identifying what went wrong. So when a French submarine (潜水艇) detected the device's homing signal five days later, the discovery marked a huge step toward determining the cause of a tragedy in which 152 passengers were killed.

In 1958, Australian scientist David Warren developed a flight-memory recorder that would track basic information like altitude and direction. That was the first mode for a black box, which became a requirement on all U.S. commercial flights by 1960. Early models often failed to withstand crashes, however, so in 1965 the device was completely redesigned and moved to the rear of the plane—the area least subject to impact—from its original position in the landing wells (起落架舱).

The same year, the Federal Aviation Authority required that the boxes, which were never actually black, be painted orange or yellow to aid visibility.

Modern airplanes have two black boxes: a voice recorder, which tracks pilots' conversations, and a flight-data recorder, which monitors fuel levels, engine noises and other operating functions that help investigators reconstruct the aircraft's final moments. Placed in an insulated (隔绝的) case and surrounded by a quarter-inch-thick panels of stainless steel, the boxes can withstand massive force and temperatures up to 2,000°F. When submerged, they're also able to emit signals from depths of 20,000 ft. Experts believe the boxes from Air France Flight 447, which crashed near Brazil on June 1, 2009, are in water nearly that deep, but statistics say they're still likely to turn up. In the approximately 20 deep-sea crashes over the past 30 years, only one plane's black boxes were never recovered.

11. What does the author say about the black box?

A) It ensures the normal functioning of an airplane.

B) The idea for its design comes from a comic book.

C) Its ability to ward off disasters is incredible.

D) It is an indispensable device on an airplane.

12. What information could be found from the black box on the Yemeni airliner?

A) Data for analyzing the cause of the crash.

B) The total number of passengers on board.

C) The scene of the crash and extent of the damage.

D) Homing signals sent by the pilot before the crash.

13. Why was the black box redesigned in 1965?

A) New materials became available by that time.

B) Too much space was needed for its installation.

C) The early models often got damaged in the crash.

D) The early models didn't provide the needed data.

14. Why did the Federal Aviation Authority require the black boxes be painted orange or yellow?

A) To distinguish them from the colour of the plane.

B) To caution people to handle them with care.

C) To make them easily identifiable.

D) To conform to international standards.

15. What do we know about the black boxes from Air France Flight 447?

A) There is still a good chance of their being recovered.

B) There is an urgent need for them to be reconstructed.

C) They have stopped sending homing signals.

D) They were destroyed somewhere near Brazil.

Passage Four

Questions 16 to 20 are based on the following passage.

It is pretty much a **one-way** street. While it may be common for university researchers to try their luck in the commercial world, there is very little traffic in the opposite direction. Pay has always been the biggest **deterrent**, as people with families often feel they cannot afford the drop in salary when moving to a university job. For some industrial scientists, however, the attractions of academia (学术界) outweigh any financial considerations.

Helen Lee took a 70% cut in salary when she moved from a senior post in Abbott Laboratories to a medical department at the University of Cambridge. Her main reason for returning to academia mid-career was to take advantage of the greater freedom to choose research questions. Some areas of inquiry have few prospects of a commercial return, and Lee's is one of them.

The impact of a salary cut is probably less severe for a scientist in the early stages of a career. Guy Grant, now a research associate at the Unilever Centre for Molecular Informatics at the University of Cambridge, spent two years working for a pharmaceutical (制药的) company before returning to university as a post-doctoral researcher. He took a 30% salary cut but felt it worthwhile for the greater intellectual opportunities.

Higher up the ladder, where a pay cut is usually more significant, the demand for scientists with a wealth of experience in industry is forcing universities to make the transition (转换) to academia more attractive, according to Lee. Industrial scientists tend to receive training that academics do not, such as how to build a multidisciplinary team, manage budgets and negotiate contracts. They are also well placed to bring something extra to the teaching side of an academic role that will help students get a job when they graduate, says Lee, perhaps experience in manufacturing practice or product development. "Only a small number of undergraduates will continue in an academic career. So someone leaving university who already has the skills needed to work in an industrial lab has far more potential in the job market than someone who has spent all their time on a narrow research project."

16. By "a one-way street" (Para. 1), the author means _____.

A) university researchers know little about the commercial world

B) there is little exchange between industry and academia

C) few industrial scientists would quit to work in a university

D) few university professors are willing to do industrial research

17. The word "deterrent" (Para. 1) most probably refers to something that _____.

A) keeps someone from taking action

B) helps to move the traffic

C) attracts people's attention

D) brings someone a financial burden

18. What was Helen Lee's major consideration when she changed her job in the middle of her career?

A) Flexible work hours.

B) Her research interests.

C) Her preference for the lifestyle on campus.

D) Prospects of academic accomplishments.

19. Guy Grant chose to work as a researcher at Cambridge in order to _____ .

A) do financially more rewarding work

B) raise his status in the academic world

C) enrich his experience in medical research

D) exploit better intellectual opportunities

20. What contribution can industrial scientists make when they come to teach in a university?

A) Increase its graduates' competitiveness in the job market.

B) Develop its students' potential in research.

C) Help it to obtain financial support from industry.

D) Gear its research towards practical applications.

Part Two: Vocabulary and Structure (35%, 1point each)

Directions: there are 40 incomplete sentences in this part. For each sentence there are four choices marked completes the sentence. Then write the corresponding letter on the **Answer Sheet**.

21. Mary's score on the test is the highest in her class; she _____ have studied very hard.

A) may

B) should

C) must

D) ought to

22. He suggested _____ to tomorrow's exhibition together.

A) us to go

B) we went

C) we shall go

D) we go

23. It's no use _____ me not to worry.

A) you tell

B) your telling

C) for you to have told

D) having told

24. Silver is the best conductor of electricity, copper _____ it closely.

A) followed

B) following

C) to follow

D) being followed

25. He went ahead _____ all warnings about the danger of his mission.

A) in case of

B) because of

C) regardless of

D) prior to

26. If these shoes are too big, ask the clerk to bring you a smaller _____.

A) suit

B) set

C) one

D) pair

27. They decided to chase the cow away _____ it did more damage.

A) unless

B) until

C) before

D) although

28. The bridge was named _____ the hero who gave his life for the cause of the people.

A) after

B) with

C) by

D) from

29. It wasn't such a good dinner _____ she had promised us.

A) that

B) which

C) as

D) what

30. We _____ our breakfast when an old man came to the door.

A) just have had

B) have just had

C) just had

D) had just had

31. It is not difficult to _____ the idea that machines may communicate information to us.

A) admit

B) receive

C) accept

D) convince

32. The socks were too small and it was only by _____ them that he managed to get them on.

A) spreading

B) extending

C) lengthening

D) stretching

33. Language can be defined as a tool by which human beings _____ with one another.

A) associate

B) connect

C) communicate

D) correspond

34. It was difficult to guess what her _____ to the news would be.

A) impression

B) reaction

C) comment

D) opinion

35. There were some _____ flowers on the table.

A) artificial

B) unnatural

C) false

D) unreal

36. Many people complain of the rapid _____ of modern life.

A) rate

B) speed

C) pace

D) growth

37. No sooner had we reached the top of the hill _____ we all sat down to rest.

A) when

B) then

C) than

D) until

38. He was _____ of having asked such a silly question.

A) sorry

B) guilty

C) ashamed

D) miserable

39. They are building the dam in _____ with another firm.

A) comparison

B) association

C) touch

D) tune

40. This bird's large wings _____ it to fly very fast.

A) able

B) enable

C) unsure

D) cause

41. You should have put the milk in the ice box; I expect it _____ undrinkable by now.

A) became

B) had become

C) has become

D) becomes

42. Codes are a way of writing something in secret; _____, anyone who doesn't know the code will not be able to read it.

A) that is

B) worse still

C) in short

D) on the other hand

43. His long service with the company was _____ with a present.

A) admitted

B) acknowledged

C) attributed

D) accepted

44. The atmosphere is as much a part of the earth as _____ its soils and the water of its lakes, rivers and oceans.

A) are

B) is

C) do

D) has

45. Our house is about a mile from the station and there are not many houses _____.

A) in between

B) among them

C) far apart

D) from each other

46. Professor smith and Professor Brown will _____ in giving the class lectures.

A) alter

B) change

C) alternate

D) differ

47. Understanding the cultural habits of another nation, especially _____ containing as many different subcultures as the United States, is a complex task.

A) one

B) the one

C) that

D) such

48. The manager promised to have my complaint _____.

A) looked through

B) looked into

C) looked over

D) looked after

49. You can't be _____ careful in making the decision as it was such a critical case.

A) very

B) quite

C) too

D) so

50. Children are _____ to have some accidents as they grow up.

A) obvious

B) indispensable

C) bound

D) doubtless

51. There is no electricity again. Has the _____ blown then?

A) fuse

B) wire

C) plug

D) circuit

52. No longer are contributions to computer technology confined to any one country; _____ is this more true than in Europe.

A) hardly

B) little

C) seldom

D) nowhere

53. The mother didn't know who _____ for the broken glass.

A) will blame

B) to blame

C) blamed

D) blames

54. Every society has its own peculiar customs and _____ of acting.

A) ways

B) attitudes

C) behavior

D) means

55. If a person talks about his weak points, his listener is expected to say something in the way of _____.

A) assurance

B) persuasion

C) encouragement

D) confirmation

Part Three: Cloze (10%, 1 point each)

Directions: There are 10 blanks in the following passage. For each blank there are four choices marked A, B, C and D. You should choose the ONE that best fits into the passage. Then mark the corresponding letter on the **Answer Sheet**.

Nobody likes insects. They are (56) _____ and sometimes dangerous. Some of them bite us and give us (57) _____; others bite us and give us big red (58) _____. Some do not bite, (59) _____ they just fly round our heads or crawl round our houses and gardens. And we do not like any of them (60) _____ those lovely butterflies.

But insects are interesting. First, they are very (61) _____ animals. Three hundred and twenty million years ago there were no men or other (62) _____ in the world but there were insects. Today, (63) _____ every square mile of land there are millions of them flying and crawling (64) _____. Second, insects are very (65) _____ to their habitat, to their food and to the weather.

56. A) wicked   B) disgusted   C) troubling   D) annoying
57. A) wounds   B) diseases   C) tumors   D) ulcers
58. A) places   B) points   C) spots   D) specks
59. A) and   B) but   C) or   D) because
60. A) besides   B) let alone   C) except for   D) except
61. A) old   B) young   C) small   D) weak
62. A) mammals   B) amphibians   C) reptiles   D) birds
63. A) on   B) with   C) throughout   D) in
64. A) over   B) above   C) about   D) up
65. A) suitable   B) adaptable   C) agreeable   D) variable

Part Four: Translation (15%, 3 points each)

Directions: *Read the following short passages carefully and translate the underlined sentences into Chinese. Please write your translation on **Answer Sheet**.*

Eating a balanced diet is important for good health. 66. <u>Many people believe that fruits and vegetables are essential parts of their meals.</u> 67. <u>Eating a variety of foods can help provide the nutrients our bodies need.</u> 68. <u>Drinking enough water is also crucial for staying hydrated.</u> 69. <u>Fast food may be convenient, but it often contains too much salt and fat.</u> 70. <u>Making healthy choices can lead to a longer and happier life.</u>

Model Test 2

Part One: Reading Comprehension (40%, 2 points each)

Direction: *There are 4 passages in this part. Each passage is followed by some questions or unfinished statements. For each of them there are four choices marked A, B, C and D. You should decide on the best choice and write the corresponding letter on **Answer Sheet**.*

Passage One
Questions 1 to 5 are based on the following passage.

It's an annual argument. Do we or do we not go on holiday? My partner says no because the boiler could go, or the roof fall off and we have no savings to save us. I say you only live once and we work hard and what's the point if you can't go on holiday. The joy of a recession means no argument next year—we just won't go.

Since money is known to be one of the things most likely to bring a relationship to its knees, we should be grateful. For many families the recession means more than not booking a holiday. A YouGov poll of 2,000 people found 22% said they were arguing more with their partners because of concerns about money. What's less clear is whether divorce and separation rates rise in a recession—financial pressures mean couples argue more but make splitting up less affordable. A recent research shows arguments about money were especially damaging to couples. Disputes were characterized by intense verbal (言语上的) aggression, tended to be repeated and not resolved and made men, more than women, extremely angry.

Kim Stephenson, an occupational psychologist, believes money is such a big deal because of what it symbolizes, which may be different things to men and women. "People can say the same things about money but have different ideas of what it's for." he explains. "They'll say it's to save to spend, for security, for freedom, to show someone you love them." He says men are more likely to see money as a way of buying status and of showing their parents that they've achieved something.

"The biggest problem is that couples assume each other know what's going on with their finances, but they don't. There seems to be more of a taboo (禁忌) about talking about money than about death. But you both need to know what you're doing, who's paying what into the joint account and how much you keep separately. In a healthy relationship, you don't have to agree about money, but you have to talk about it."

1. What does the author say about vacationing?

A) People enjoy it all the more during a recession.

B) Few people can afford it without working hard.

C) It makes all the hard work worthwhile.

D) It is the chief cause of family disputes.

2. What does the author mean by saying "money is known…to bring a relationship to its knees" (Para. 2)?

A) Money is considered to be the root of all evils.

B) Some people sacrifice their dignity for money.

C) Few people can resist the temptation of money.

D) Disputes over money may ruin a relationship.

3. The YouGov poll of 2,000 people indicates that in a recession _____.

A) conflicts between couples tend to rise

B) it is more expensive for couples to split up

C) couples show more concern for each other

D) divorce and separation rates increase

4. What does Kim Stephenson believe?

A) Money is often a symbol of a person's status.

B) Money means a great deal to both and women.

C) Men and women spend money on different things.

D) Men and women view money in different ways.

5. The author suggests at the end of the passage that couples should _____.

A) put their money together instead of keeping it separately

B) make efforts to reach agreement on their family budgets

C) discuss money matters to maintain a healthy relationship

D) avoid arguing about money matters to remain romantic

Passage Two

Questions 6 to 10 are based on the following passage.

In times of economic crisis. Americans turn to their families for support. If the Great Depression is any guide, we may see a drop in our skyhigh divorce rate. But this won't necessarily represent. an increase in happy marriages. In the long run, the Depression weakened American families, and the current crisis will probably do the same.

We tend to think of the Depression as a time when families pulled together to survive huge job losses. By 1932, when nearly one-quarter of the workforce was unemployed, the divorce rate had declined by around 25% from 1929. But this doesn't mean people were suddenly happier with their marriages. Rather, with incomes decreasing and insecure jobs, unhappy couples often couldn't afford to divorce. They feared neither spouse could manage alone.

Today, given the job losses of the past year, fewer unhappy couples will risk starting separate households. Furthermore, the housing market meltdown will make it more difficult for them to finance their separations by selling their homes.

After financial disasters family members also tend to do whatever they can to help each other and their communities. A 1940 book, *The Unemployed Man and His Family*, described a family in which the husband initially reacted to losing his job "with tireless search for work." He was always active, looking for odd jobs to do.

The problem is that such an impulse is hard to sustain. Across the country, many similar families were unable to maintain the initial boost in morale（士气）. For some, the hardships of life without steady work eventually overwhelmed their attempts to keep their families together. The divorce rate rose again during the rest of the decade as the recovery took hold.

Millions of American families may now be in the initial stage of their responses to the current crisis, working together and supporting one another through the early months of unemployment.

Today's economic crisis could well generate a similar number of couples whose relationships have been irreparably（无法弥补地）ruined. So it's only when the economy is healthy again that we'll begin to see just how many broken families have been created.

6. In the initial stage, the current economic crisis is likely to _____.

A) tear many troubled families apart

B) contribute to enduring family ties

C) bring about a drop in the divorce rate

D) cause a lot of conflicts in the family

7. In the Great Depression many unhappy couples close to stick together because _____.

A) starting a new family would be hard

B) they expected things would turn better

C) they wanted to better protect their kids

D) living separately would be too costly

8. In addition to job losses, what stands in the way of unhappy couples getting a divorce?

A) Mounting family debts.

B) A sense of insecurity.

C) Difficulty in getting a loan.

D) Falling housing prices.

9. What will the current economic crisis eventually do to some married couples?

A) It will force them to pull their efforts together.

B) It will undermine their mutual understanding.

C) It will help strengthen their emotional bonds.

D) It will irreparably damage their relationship.

10. What can be inferred from the last paragraph?

A) The economic recovery will see a higher divorce rate.

B) Few couples can stand the test of economic hardships.

C) A stable family is the best protection against poverty.

D) Money is the foundation of many a happy marriage.

Passage Three

Questions 11 to 15 are based on the following passage.

As you are probably aware, the latest job markets news isn't good: Unemployment is still more than 9 percent, and new job growth has fallen close to zero. That's bad for the economy, of course. And it may be especially discouraging if you happen to be looking for a job or hoping to change careers right now. But it actually shouldn't matter to you nearly as much as you think.

That's because job growth numbers don't matter to job hunters as much as job turnover (人员更替) data. After all, existing jobs open up every day due to promotions, resignations, terminations (解雇), and retirements. (Yes, people are retiring even in this economy.) In both good times and bad, turnover creates more openings than economic growth does. Even in June of 2007, when the economy was still moving ahead, job growth was only 132,000, while turnover was 4.7 million!

And as it turns out, even today — with job growth near zero — over 4 million job hunters are being hired every month.

I don't mean to imply that overall job growth doesn't have an impact on one's ability to land a job. It's true that if total employment were higher, it would mean more jobs for all of us to choose from (and compete for). And it's true that there are currently more people applying for each available job opening, regardless of whether it's a new one or not.

But what often distinguishes those who land jobs from those who don't is their ability to stay motivated. They're willing to do the hard work of identifying their valuable skills; be creative about where and how to look; learn how to present themselves to potential employers; and keep going, even after repeated rejections. The Bureau of Labor Statistics data shows that 2.7 million people who wanted and were available for work hadn't looked within the last four weeks and were no longer even classified as unemployed.

So don't let the headlines fool you into giving up. Four million people get hired every month in the U.S. You can be one of them.

11. The author tends to believe that high unemployment rate _____.

A) deprives many people of job opportunities

B) prevents many people from changing careers

C) should not stop people from looking for a job

D) does not mean the U. S. economy is worsening

12. Where do most job openings come from?

A) Job growth.

B) Job turnover.

C) Improved economy.

D) Business expansion.

13. What does the author say about overall job growth?

A) It doesn't have much effect on individual job seekers.

B) It increases people's confidence in the economy.

C) It gives a ray of hope to the unemployed.

D) It doesn't mean greater job security for the employed.

14. What is the key to landing a job according to the author?

A) Education.

B) Intelligence.

C) Persistence.

D) Experience.

15. What do we learn from the passage about the unemployment figures in the U. S. ?

A) They clearly indicate how healthy the economy is.

B) They provide the public with the latest information.

C) They warn of the structural problems in the economy.

D) They exclude those who have stopped looking for a job.

Passage Four

Questions 16 to 20 are based on the following passage.

It's no secret that some of the resolutions that many of us vowed to pursue in the new year—eat healthy, lose weight, quit smoking, save more money—have already fallen by the wayside.

Many of them are likely the same resolutions that we abandoned last January. And it's a good thing for whose who sell health club memberships, quit-smoking programs and other products that help us think we can improve our lives.

Many gyms see new memberships double in January, making up for the third of their members who do not renew each year.

And many who sign up in January will be no-shows by February.

"If I try one quick fix and it doesn't work, I may be more likely to try the next quick fix," Lisa

Lahey, who coaches executives how to sustain behavior change, told *The Times*.

The Biggest Loser Resort at Fitness Ridge doesn't offer any quick fixes, just a 12-hour schedule full of exercise, a 1,200-calories-a-day diet and a fee of $2,000 a week. The resort teaches its clients that "weight management" is a combination of fitness, diet and emotional health.

"Given my recent weight gain, and the fact that I was turning 50," Jennifer Conlin wrote in *The Times*, "I wanted to start a program that would make 2012 the year I finally got in shape."

"For years, the advice to the overweight people has been that we simply need to eat less ad exercise more," Tara Parker-Pope wrote. "While there is truth to this guidance, it fails to take into account that the human body continues to fight against weight loss long after dieting has stopped. This translates into a sobering (令人清醒的) reality: once we become fat, most of us, despite our best efforts, will probably stay fat."

Of course this revelation (揭示), if proven true by further study, is not good news for the weight-loss industry. But chances are it won't have much impact on the human tendency to resolve to get to the gym more and avoid chocolate cake when the clock strikes midnight on December 31.

16. What do we learn from the first paragraph about new year resolutions?

A) They are hard to sustain.

B) They test one's strength.

C) They help shed bad habits.

D) They promise a good year.

17. Who do new year resolutions eventually benefit?

A) Society in general.

B) Business executives.

C) Health club members.

D) Health industries.

18. What is special about the Biggest Loser Resort's weight management program?

A) It gives top priority to emotional health.

B) It does not resort to any quick fixes.

C) It focuses on one's behavior change.

D) It is not cheap but extremely effective.

19. What happens when people stop dieting?

A) They regain their appetite.

B) They usually stay in shape.

C) They weight bounces back.

D) Their health is likely to fail.

20. What do people tend to do about new year resolutions?

A) They keep making them year after year.

B) They abandon them once progress is made.

C) They keep trying until they finally succeed.

D) They make them for the sake of making them.

Part Two: Vocabulary and Structure (35%, 1 point each)

Directions: there are 40 incomplete sentences in this part. For each sentence there are four choices marked completes the sentence. Then write the corresponding letter on the **Answer Sheet**.

21. What _____ to him is whether the job allows him to pursue his studies.

A) refers

B) matters

C) happens

D) applies

22. It was unwise of him to _____ the unreliable data in his speech.

A) add to

B) refer to

C) keep to

D) point to

23. Many Europeans _____ the continent of Africa in the 19th century.

A) exploded

B) explored

C) exposed

D) expanded

24. _____ its hot sun and beautiful beaches, Hawaii is a fine place to live in or to visit.

A) As

B) With

C) From

D) For

25. There are certain _____ when you must interrupt people who are in the middle of doing something.

A) conditions

B) situations

C) occasions

D) environments

26. If you happen to _____ my lost papers while you're looking for your book, please let me know at once by telephone.

A) properly

B) come up

C) come to

D) come across

27. Her fluency in English gives her an advantage _____ other girls for the job.

A) above

B) over

C) than

D) with

28. What he told us about the affair simply doesn't make any _____.

A) significance

B) idea

C) meaning

D) sense

29. There were beautiful clothes _____ in the shop windows.

A) spread

B) displayed

C) exposed

D) located

30. Franklin's ability to learn from observations and experience _____ greatly to his success in public life.

A) contributed

B) owed

C) attached

D) related

31. By the end of this month, we surely _____ a satisfactory solution to the problem.

A) have found

B) will be finding

C) will have found

D) are finding

32. They usually have less money at the end of the month than _____ at the beginning.

A) which is

B) which was

C) they have

D) it is

33. In the course of a day students do far more than just _____ classes.

A) attend

B) attended

C) to attend

D) attending

34. We regret to inform you that the materials you ordered are _____ .

A) out of work

B) out of stock

C) out of reach

D) out of practice

35. Could you find someone _____ .

A) for me to play tennis with

B) for me to play tennis

C) play tennis with

D) playing tennis with

36. The manager of the hotel requests that their guests _____ after 11:00 p.m.

A) not to play loud music

B) shouldn't play loud music

C) don't play loud music

D) couldn't play loud music

37. The Browns _____ here, but not any more.

A) were used to living

B) had lived

C) used to live

D) had been living

38. After searching for half an hour she realized that her glasses _____ on the table all the time.

A) were lain

B) had been lain

C) had been lying

D) would have been lying

39. Hardly _____ the helicopter _____ when the waiting crowd ran toward it.

A) has…landed

B) had…landed

C) would…land

D) was…landing

40. Jane was fairly good at English, but in mathematics she could not _____ the rest of the students in her class.

A) put up with

B) do away with

C) keep up with

D) run away with

41. The girl is so sensitive that she is _____ to get angry at the slightest offence.

A) adaptable

B) liable

C) fit

D) suitable

42. He was at the _____ of his career when he was murdered.

A) glory

B) power

C) pride

D) height

43. I have never met the professor though I have been in correspondence _____ him for several years.

A) with

B) by

C) of

D) to

44. _____ they must learn in a course is not provided in the classroom.

A) Many things

B) So much

C) Much of what

D) All what

45. Of the immigrants who came to America in the first three quarters of the seventeenth century, the _____ majority was English.

A) overwhelming

B) overflowing

C) overtaking

D) overloading

46. By the first decade of the 21st century, international commercial air traffic is expected _____ vastly beyond today's levels.

A) to have extended

B) to be extending

C) being extended

D) having been extended

47. The doctor warned his patient that _____ should he return to work until he had completely recovered.

A) on all accounts

B) on no account

C) on any account

D) on every account

48. We started burning some leaves in our yard, but the fire got _____ and we had to call the fire department to put it out.

A) out of hand

B) out of order

C) out of the question

D) out of the way

49. If an earthquake occurred, some of the one-storey houses _____ .

A) might be standing left

B) might be left standing

C) might leave to be standing

D) might be left to stand

50. The professor picked several students _____ from the class and asked them to help him with the experiment.

A) at ease

B) at all

C) at random

D) at hand

51. Though I've never seen you before. I guess you _____ be the new secretary.

A) should

B) must

C) would

D) could

52. This store has an excellent _____ for fair dealing.

A) repetition

B) reputation

C) authority

D) popularity

53. The atmosphere is as much a part of the earth as _____ its soils and the water of its lakes, rivers and oceans.

A) has

B) do

C) is

D) are

54. Her terror was so great _____ somewhere to escape, she would have run for her life.

A) only if there had been

B) that there had only been

C) that had there only been

D) if there was only

55. While you pedal away on the exercise bicycle, a machine will be _____ your breathing and pulse.

A) reviewing

B) screening

C) surveying

D) monitoring

Part Three: Cloze (10%, 1 point each)

Directions: *There are 10 blanks in the following passage. For each blank there are four choices marked A, B, C and D. You should choose the ONE that best fits into the passage. Then mark the corresponding letter on the **Answer Sheet**.*

Exercise is good for you, but most people really know very little about how to exercise properly. (56) _____ when you try, you can run into trouble. Many people (57) _____ that when specific muscles are exercised, the fat in the neighbouring area is "(58) _____ up". Yet the (59) _____ is that exercise burns fat from all over the (60) _____.

Studies show muscles which are not (61) _____ lose their strength very quickly. To regain it needs 48 to 72 hours and exercise every other day will (62) _____ a normal level of physical strength. To (63) _____ weight you should always "work up a good sweat" when exercising. (64) _____ sweating only (65) _____ body temperature to prevent over heating.

56. A) While	B) When	C) As	D) So
57. A) understand	B) believe	C) hope	D) know
58. A) built	B) burned	C) piled	D) grown
59. A) reply	B) possibility	C) truth	D) reason
60. A) arm	B) leg	C) stomach	D) body
61. A) exercised	B) examined	C) protected	D) cured
62. A) boil	B) raise	C) burn	D) keep
63. A) lose	B) gain	C) reap	D) burn
64. A) Certainly	B) But	C) Fortunately	D) Probably
65. A) raises	B) reduces	C) destroys	D) keeps up

Part Four: Translation (15%, 3 points each)

Directions: *Read the following short passages carefully and translate the underlined sentences into Chinese. Please write your translation on **Answer Sheet**.*

Reading books has many benefits. 66. <u>It can improve your vocabulary and language skills.</u> 67. <u>People who read regularly often have better focus and concentration.</u> 68. <u>Reading can also reduce stress and help you relax.</u> 69. <u>You can learn about different cultures and ideas through books.</u> 70. <u>Overall, making time for reading is a good habit to develop.</u>

Model Test 3

Part One: Reading Comprehension (40%, 2 points each)

Direction: *There are 4 passages in this part. Each passage is followed by some questions or unfinished statements. For each of them there are four choices marked A, B, C and D. You should decide on the best choice and write the corresponding letter on* **Answer Sheet**.

Passage One
Questions 1 to 5 are based on the following passage.

The Gatais used to frown when they received power bills that routinely topped $200. Last September the couple moved into a 1,500-square-foot home in Premier Gardens, a subdivision of 95 "zero-energy homes" (ZEH) just outside town. Now they're actually eager to see their electricity bills. The grand total over the 10 months they've lived in the three-bedroom house: $75. For the past two months they haven't paid a cent.

ZEH communities are the leading edge of technologies that might someday create houses that produce as much energy as they consume. Premier Gardens is one of a half-dozen subdivisions in California where every home cuts power consumption by 50%, mostly by using low-power appliances and solar panels.

Aside from the panels on the roof, Premier Gardens looks like a community of conventional homes. But inside, special windows cut power bills by blocking solar heat in summer and retaining indoor warmth in winter.

The rest of the energy savings comes from the solar units. They don't just feed the home they serve. If they generate more power than the home is using, the excess flows into the utility's power grid (电网). The residents are billed by "net metering": they pay for the amount of power they tap off the grid, less the kilowatts (千瓦) they feed into it. If a home generates more power than it uses, the bill is zero.

That sounds like a bad deal for the power company, but it's not. Solar homes produce the most power on the hot sunny afternoons when everyone rushes home to turn up the air conditioner. "It helps us lower usage at peak power times," says solar expert Mike Keesee. "That lets us avoid building costly plants or buying expensive power at peak usage time."

What's not to like? Mostly the costs. The special features can add $25,000 or more to the purchase price of a house. Tax breaks bring the cost down, especially in California, but in many states ZEHs can be prohibitively expensive. For the consumer, it's a matter of paying now for the hardware to save later on the utilities.

1. Why are the Gatais eager to see their electricity bills now?

A) They want to see how much they have saved.

B) They want to cut down their utility expenses.

C) They want to know if they are able to pay.

D) They want to avoid being overcharged.

2. What is special about the ZEH communities?

A) They have created cutting-edge technologies.

B) They aim to be self-sufficient in power supply.

C) They are subdivided into half a dozen sections.

D) They are built in harmony with the environment.

3. How are the residents in the ZEH communities billed for electricity use?

A) They are only charged for the amount of power they consume on rainy days.

B) They needn't pay a single cent for their power consumption on sunny days.

C) They only pay for the excess power that flows into the utility's power grid.

D) They pay for the electricity from the grid less their home-generated power.

4. What does the "net metering" practice mean to the power company?

A) More pressure at peak time.

C) Increased electricity output.

B) Less profits in the short term.

D) Reduced operational costs.

5. The author believes that buying a house in a ZEH community _____.

A) is but a dream for average consumers

B) gives the owner substantial tax benefits

C) is a worthy investment in the long run

D) contributes to environmental protection

Passage Two

Questions 6 to 10 are based on the following passage.

Junk food is everywhere, we're eating too much of it. Most of us know what we're doing and yet we do it anyway. So here's a suggestion offered by two researchers at the Rand Corporation: Why not take a lesson from alcohol control policies and apply them to where food is sold and how it's displayed?

"Many policy measures to control obesity (肥胖症) assume that people consciously and rationally choose what and how much they eat and therefore focus on providing information and more access to healthier foods," note the two researchers. "In contrast," the researchers continue, "many regulations that don't assume people make rational choices have been successfully applied to control alcohol, a substance like food—of which immoderate consumption leads to serious health problems."

The research references studies of people's behavior with food and alcohol and results of alcohol restrictions, and then lists five regulations that the researchers think might be promising if applied to junk foods. Among them: Density restrictions: licenses to sell alcohol aren't handed out unplanned to all comers but are allotted (分配) based on the number of places in an area that already sell alcohol. These make alcohol less easy to get and reduce the number of psychological cues to drink.

Similarly, the researchers say, being presented with junk food stimulates our desire to eat it. So why not limit the density of food outlets, particularly ones that sell food rich in empty calories? And why not limit sale of food in places that aren't primarily food stores?

Display and sales restrictions: California has a rule prohibiting alcohol displays near the cash registers in gas stations, and in most places you can't buy alcohol at drive-through facilities. At supermarkets, food companies pay to have their wares in places where they're easily seen. One could remove junk food to the back of the store and ban them from the shelves at checkout lines. The other measures include restricting portion sizes, taxing and prohibiting special price deals for junk foods, and placing warning labels on the products.

6. What does the author say about junk food?

A) People should be educated not to eat too much.

B) It is widely consumed despite its ill reputation.

C) Its temptation is too strong for people to resist.

D) It causes more harm than is generally realized.

7. What do the Rand researchers think of many of the policy measures to control obesity?

A) They should be implemented effectively.

B) They provide misleading information.

C) They are based on wrong assumptions.

D) They help people make rational choices.

8. Why do policymakers of alcohol control place density restrictions?

A) Few people are able to resist alcohol's temptations.

B) There are already too many stores selling alcohol.

C) Drinking strong alcohol can cause social problems.

D) Easy access leads to customers' over-consumption.

9. What is the purpose of California's rule about alcohol display in gas stations?

A) To effectively limit the density of alcohol outlets.

B) To help drivers to give up the habit of drinking.

C) To prevent possible traffic jams in nearby areas.

D) To get alcohol out of drivers' immediate sight.

10. What is the general guideline the Rand researchers suggest about junk food control?

A) Guiding people to make rational choices about food.

B) Enhancing people's awareness of their own health.

C) Borrowing ideas from alcohol control measures.

D) Resorting to economic, legal and psychological means.

Passage Three

Questions 11 to 15 are based on the following passage.

Reading leadership literature, you'd sometimes think that everyone has the potential to be an effective leader.

I don't believe that to be true. In fact, I see fewer truly effective leaders than I see people stuck in positions of leadership who are sadly incompetent and seriously misguided about their own abilities.

Part of the reason this happens is a lack of honest self-assessment by those who aspire to（追求）leadership in the first place.

We've all met the type of Individual who simply must take charge. Whether it's a decision-making session, a basketball game, or a family outing, they can't help grabbing the lead dog position and clinging on to it for dear life. They believe they're natural born leaders.

Truth is, they're nothing of the sort. True leaders don't assume that it's their divine（神圣的）right to take charge every time two or more people get together. Quite the opposite. A great leader will assess each situation on its merits, and will only take charge when their position, the situation, and/or the needs of the moment demand it.

Many business executives confuse leadership with action. They believe that constant motion somehow generates leadership as a byproduct. Faced with any situation that can't be solved by the sheer force of activity, they generate a dust cloud of impatience. Their one leadership tool is volume: if they think you aren't working as hard as they think you should, their demands become increasingly louder and harsher. True leaders understand the value of action, of course, but it isn't their only tool. In fact, it isn't even their primary tool. Great leaders see more than everyone else: answers, solutions, patterns, problems, opportunities. They know it's vitally important to do, but they also know that thinking, understanding, reflection and interpretation are equally important.

If you're too concerned with outcomes to the extent that you manipulate and intimidate others to achieve those outcomes, then you aren't leading at all, you're dictating. A true leader is someone who develops his or her team so that they can and do hit their targets and achieve their goals.

11. What does the author think of the leaders he knows?

A) Many of them are used to taking charge.

B) Few of them are equal to their positions.

C) Many of them fail to fully develop their potential.

D) Few of them are familiar with leadership literature.

12. Why are some people eager to grab leadership positions?

A) They believe they have the natural gift to lead.

B) They believe in what leadership literature says.

C) They have proved competent in many situations.

D) They derive great satisfaction from being leaders.

13. What characterizes a great leader according to the author?

A) Being able to take prompt action when chances present themselves.

B) Having a whole-hearted dedication to their divine responsibilities.

C) Having a full understanding of their own merits and weaknesses.

D) Being able to assess the situation carefully, before taking charge.

14. How will many business executives respond when their command fails to generate action?

A) They reassess the situation at hand.

B) They become impatient and rude.

C) They resort to any tool available.

D) They blame their team members.

15. What is the author's advice to leaders?

A) Concentrate on one specific task at a time.

B) Use different tools to achieve different goals.

C) Build up a strong mare to achieve their goals.

D) Show determination when faced with tough tasks.

Passage Four

Questions 16 to 20 are based on the following passage.

Romantic love has clear evolutionary roots but our views about what makes an ideal romantic relationship can be swayed by the society we live in. So says psychologist Maureen O'sullivan from the University of San Francisco. She suggests that humans have always tried to strengthen the pair-bond to maximize (使最大化) reproductive success.

Many societies throughout history and around the world today have cultivated strong pressures to stay married. In those where ties to family and community are strong, lifelong marriages can be promoted by practices such as the cultural prohibition of divorce and arranged marriages that are seen as a contract between two families, not just two individuals. In modern western societies, however, the focus on individuality and independence means that people are less concerned about conforming to (遵守) the dictates of family and culture. In the absence of societal pressures to maintain pair-bonds, O'sullivan suggests that romantic love has increasingly come to be seen as the factor that should determine who we stay with and for how long. "That's why historically we see an increase in romantic love as a basis for forming long-term relationships," she says.

According to O'sullivan culture also shapes the sorts of feelings we expect to have, and actually do experience, when in love. Although the negative emotions associated with romantic love—fear of loss, disappointment and jealousy—are fairly consistent across cultures, the positive feelings can vary. "If you ask Japanese students to list the positive attributes they expect in a romantic partner, they rate highly things like loyalty, commitment and devotion," says O'sullivan. "If you ask American college women, they expect everything under the sun: in addition to being committed, partners have to be amusing, funny and a friend."

We judge a potential partner according to our specific cultural expectations about what romantic love should feel like. If you believe that you have found true romance, and your culture tells you that this is what a long-term relationship should be based on, there is less need to rely on social or family pressures to keep couples together, O'sullivan argues.

16. What does the author say about people's views of an ideal romantic relationship?

A) They vary from culture to culture.

B) They ensure the reproductive success.

C) They reflect the evolutionary process.

D) They are influenced by psychologists.

17. We can infer from the passage that strong family and community ties _____.

A) largely rely on marriage contracts

B) can contribute to stable marriages

C) often run counter to romantic love

D) make divorces virtually unacceptable

18. Without social pressures to keep pair-bonds, romantic love _____.

A) will be a substitute for marriage in human relationships

B) plays a key role in maintaining long-term relationships

C) is likely to replace the dictates of family and society

D) is a way to develop individuality and independence

19. O'sullivan believes that when people from different cultures fall in love, _____.

A) they expect different things from their partner

B) they tend to exaggerate each other's positive qualities

C) they often fail to see each other's negative qualities

D) they lay more emphasis on commitment and devotion

20. We can conclude from the passage that _____.

A) cultural differences often tear apart a family built on romantic love

B) marriages are hard to sustain without social or family pressures

C) romantic love is becoming increasingly important in family relationships

D) romantic love tends to yield where family or social pressures are strong

Part Two: Vocabulary and Structure (35%, 1 point each)

Directions: there are 40 incomplete sentences in this part. For each sentence there are four choices marked completes the sentence. Then write the corresponding letter on the **Answer Sheet**.

21. _____ for my illness I would have lent him a helping hand.

A) Not being

B) Had it not been

C) Without being

D) Not having been

22. _____ a teacher in a university, it is necessary to have at least a master's degree.

A) To become

B) Become

C) One become

D) On becoming

23. Not that John doesn't want to help you, _____ it's beyond his power.

A) but that

B) for that

C) and that

D) in that

24. To be frank, I'd rather you _____ in the case.

A) will not be involved

B) not involved

C) not to be involved

D) were not involved

25. He thought that _____.

A) the effort doing the job was not worth

B) the effort was not worth in doing the job

C) it was not worth the effort doing the job

D) it was not worth the effort by doing the job

26. I would appreciate _____ it a secret.

A) your keeping

B) you to keep

C) that you keep

D) that you will keep

27. It is recommended that the project _____ until all the preparations have been made.

A) is not started

B) will not be started

C) not be started

D) is not to be started

28. We didn't know his telephone number, otherwise we _____ him.

A) would have telephoned

B) must have telephoned

C) would telephone

D) had telephoned

29. I walked too much yesterday and _____ are still aching now.

A) my leg's muscles

B) my muscles of leg

C) my leg muscles

D) my muscles of the leg

30. The destruction of these treasures was a loss for mankind that no amount of money could _____ .

A) stand up to

B) make up for

C) come up with

D) put up with

31. She was so _____ in her job that she didn't hear anybody knocking at the door.

A) attracted

B) absorbed

C) drawn

D) concentrated

32. Although I like the appearance of the house, what really made me decide to buy it was the beautiful _____ through the window.

A) vision

B) look

C) picture

D) view

33. They took _____ measures to prevent poisonous gases from escaping.

A) fruitful

B) beneficial

C) valid

D) effective

34. In developing countries people are _____ into overcrowded cities in great numbers.

A) breaking

B) filling

C) pouring

D) hurrying

35. It is quite necessary for a qualified teacher to have good manners and _____ knowledge.

A) extensive

B) expansive

C) intensive

D) expensive

36. A healthy life is frequently thought to be _____ with the open countryside and homegrown food.

A) tied

B) bound

C) involved

D) associated

37. Features such as height, weight, and skin color _____ from individual to individual and from face to face.

A) change

B) vary

C) alter

D) convert

38. A well-written composition _____ good choice of words and clear organization among other things.

A) calls on

B) calls for

C) calls up

D) calls off

39. Young adults _____ older people are more likely to prefer pop songs.

A) other than

B) more than

C) less than

D) rather than

40. Lightning is a _____ of electrical current from a cloud to the ground or from one cloud to another.

A) rush

B) rainbow

C) rack

D) ribbon

41. Tom _____ better than to ask Dick for help.

A) shall know

B) shouldn't know

C) has known

D) should have known

42. The magician picked several persons _____ from the audience and asked them to help him with the performance.

A) by accident

B) at random

C) on occasion

D) on average

43. Water enters into a great variety of chemical reactions, _____ have been mentioned in previous pages.

A) a few of it

B) a few of that

C) a few of them

D) a few of which

44. They'll have you _____ if you don't pay your taxes.

A) to be arrested

B) arrest

C) arrested

D) being arrested

45. There was a knock at the door. It was the second time someone _____ me that evening.

A) had interrupted

B) would have interrupted

C) to have interrupted

D) to interrupted

46. _____ for your help, we'd never have been able to get over the difficulties.

A) Had it not

B) If it were not

C) Had it not been

D) If we had not been

47. Some people either _____ avoid questions of right and wrong or remain neutral about them.

A) violently

B) enthusiastically

C) sincerely yours

D) deliberately

48. There is no easy solution to Japan's labour _____ .

A) decline

B) vacancy

C) rarity

D) shortage

49. I'm sure your suggestion will _____ the problem.

A) contribute to solving

B) contribute to solve

C) be contributed to solve

D) be contributed to solving

50. I left for the office earlier than usual this morning _____ traffic jam.

A) in line with

B) for the sake of

C) in case of

D) at the risk of

51. The new washing machines are _____ at the rate of fifty a day.

A) turned up

B) turned down

C) turned out

D) turned in

52. On turning the corner, we saw the road _____ steeply.

A) departing

B) descending

C) decreasing

D) depressing

53. The managing director took the _____ for the accident, although it was not really his fault.

A) guilt

B) blame

C) charge

D) accusation

54. Once they had fame, fortune, secure futures; _____ is utter poverty.

A) now that all is left

B) now all that is left

C) now all which is left

D) now all what is left

55. The shop-assistant was straight with his customers. If an article was of _____ quality he'd tell them so.

A) humble

B) inferior

C) minor

D) awkward

Part Three: Cloze (10%, 1 point each)

Directions: There are 10 blanks in the following passage. For each blank there are four choices marked A, B, C and D. You should choose the ONE that best fits into the passage. Then mark the corresponding letter on the Answer Sheet.

The translator must have an excellent up-to-date knowledge of his (56) _____ languages, full facility in the handling of his target language, which will be his mother tongue or language of habitual (57) _____, and a knowledge and understanding of the latest subject-matter in his field of (58) _____. This is, as it were, his professional equipment. (59) _____ this, it is desirable that he should have a(n) (60) _____ mind, wide interests, a good memory and the ability to grasp quickly the basic principles of new developments. He should be willing to work (61) _____ his own, often at high speeds, but should be humble enough to consult others

(62) _____ his own knowledge not always prove adequate to the task (63) _____ hand. He should be able to type fairly quickly and accurately and, if he is working mainly for publication, should have more than a nodding (64) _____ with printing techniques and proof-reading. If he is working basically as an information translator, let us say, for an industrial firm, he should have the flexibility of mind to enable him to (65) _____ rapidly from one source language to another, as well as from one subject-matter to another.

56. A) first   B) mother   C) source   D) resource
57. A) application   B) use   C) utility   D) usage
58. A) specialization B) specialist   C) specification   D) major
59. A) In addition to B) Except   C) Because of   D) Despite
60. A) experimental   B) thinking   C) inquiring   D) asking
61. A) of   B) by   C) for   D) on
62. A) when   B) because   C) if   D) should
63. A) with   B) in   C) of   D) by
64. A) familiarity   B) skill   C) acquaintance   D) contact
65. A) change   B) turn   C) transform   D) switch

Part Four: Translation (15%, 3 points each)

Directions: Read the following short passages carefully and translate the underlined sentences into Chinese. Please write your translation on **Answer Sheet**.

Exercise is vital for maintaining good health. 66. Regular physical activity can help you control your weight. 67. It also strengthens your muscles and bones. 68. Many studies show that exercise can improve your mood and reduce anxiety. 69. You don't need to spend hours at the gym; even short walks can be beneficial. 70. Staying active is an important part of a healthy lifestyle.

Model Test 4

Part One: Reading Comprehension (40%, 2 points each)

Direction: There are 4 passages in this part. Each passage is followed by some questions or unfinished statements. For each of them there are four choices marked A, B, C and D. You should decide on the best choice and write the corresponding letter on **Answer Sheet**.

Passage One

Questions 1 to 5 are based on the following passage.

Hospitals, hoping to curb medical error, have invested heavily to put computers, smartphones and other devices into the hands of medical staff for instant access to patient data, drug information and case studies.

But like many cures, this solution has come with an unintended side effect: doctors and nurses can be focused on the screen and not the patient, even during moments of critical care. A poll showed that half of medical technicians had admitted texting during a procedure.

This phenomenon has set off an intensifying discussion at hospitals and medical schools about a problem perhaps best described as "distracted doctoring". In response, some hospitals have begun limiting the use of electronic devices in critical settings, while schools have started reminding medical students to focus on patients instead of devices.

"You justify carrying devices around the hospital to do medical records, but you can surf the Internet or do Facebook, and sometimes Facebook is more tempting." said Dr. Peter Papadakos at the University of Rochester Medical Center.

"My gut feeling (本能的感觉) is lives are in danger," said Dr. Papadakos. "We're not educating people about the problem, and it's getting worse."

A survey of 439 medical technicians found that 55 percent of technicians who monitor bypass machines acknowledged that they had talked on cellphones during heart surgery. Half said they had texted while in surgery. The study concluded, "Such distractions have the potential to be disastrous."

Medical professionals have always faced interruptions from cellphones, and multitasking is simply a fact of life for many medical jobs. What has changed, say doctors, especially younger ones, is that they face increasing pressure to interact with their devices.

The pressure stems from a mantra (信条) of modern medicine that patient care must be "data driven", and informed by the latest, instantly accessible information. By many accounts, the technology has helped reduce medical error by providing instant access to patient data or prescription details.

Dr. Peter Carmel, president of the American Medical Association, said technology "offers great potential in health care", but he added that doctors, first priority should be with the patient.

1. Why do hospitals equip their staff with computers, smartphones and other devices?

A) To reduce medical error.

B) To cope with emergencies.

C) To facilitate administration.

D) To simplify medical procedures.

2. What does the author refer to by "distracted doctoring"?

A) The disservice done by modem devices to doctors, nurses, as well as patients.

B) The tendency of medical institutions encouraging the use of modem devices.

C) The problem of devices preventing doctors from focusing on their patients.

D) The phenomenon of medical staff attending to personal affairs while working.

3. What does Dr. Peter Papadakos worry about?

A) Medical students are not adequately trained to use modern technology.

B) Doctors' interaction with their devices may endanger patients, lives.

C) Doctors are relying too heavily on modern electronic technology.

D) Pressures on the medical profession may become overwhelming.

4. Why do doctors feel increasing pressure to use modern devices?

A) Patients trust doctors who use modern technology.

B) Use of modern devices adds hospitals' revenues.

C) Data is given too much importance in patient care.

D) Patients' data has to be revised from time to time.

5. What is Peter Carmel's advice to doctors?

A) They follow closely the advances in medical science.

B) They focus their attention on the patient's condition.

C) They observe hospital rules and regulations.

D) They make the best use of modem devices.

Passage Two

Questions 6 to 10 are based on the following passage.

The rise of the Internet has been one of the most transformative developments in human history, comparable in impact to the invention of the printing press and the telegraph. Over two billion people worldwide now have access to vastly more information than ever before, and can communicate with each other instantly, often using Web-connected mobile devices they carry everywhere. But the Internets tremendous impact has only just begun.

"Mass adoption of the Internet is driving one of the most exciting social, cultural, and political transformations in history, and unlike earlier periods of change, this time the effects are fully global," Schmidt and Cohen write in their new book, *The New Digital Age*.

Perhaps the most profound changes will come when the five billion people worldwide who currently lack Internet access get online. The authors do an excellent job of examining the implications of the Internet revolution for individuals, governments, and institutions like the news media. But if the book has one major shortcoming, it's that the authors don't spend enough time applying a critical eye to the role of Internet businesses in these sweeping changes.

In their book, the authors provide the most authoritative volume to date that describes—and more importantly predicts—how the Internet will shape our lives in the coming decades. They paint a picture of a world in which individuals, companies, institutions, and governments must deal with two realities, one physical, and one virtual.

At the core of the book is the idea that "technology is neutral, but people aren't." By using this concept as a starting point, the authors aim to move beyond the now familiar optimist vs. pessimist dichotomy (对立观点) that has characterized many recent debates about whether the rise of the Internet will ultimately be good or bad for society. In an interview with *TIME* earlier this week, Cohen said although he and his co-author are optimistic about many aspects of the Internet, they've also realistic about the risks and dangers that lie ahead when the next five billion people come online, particularly with respect to personal privacy and state surveillance (监视).

6. In what way is the rise of the Internet similar to the invention of the printing press and the telegraph?

A) It transforms human history.

B) It facilitates daily communication.

C) It is adopted by all humanity.

D) It revolutionizes people's thinking.

7. How do Schmidt and Cohen describe the effects of the Internet?

A) They are immeasurable.

B) They are worldwide.

C) They are unpredictable.

D) They are contaminating.

8. In what respect is the book *The New Digital Age* considered inadequate?

A) It fails to recognize the impact of the Internet technology.

B) It fails to look into the social implications of the Internet.

C) It lacks an objective evaluation of the role of Internet businesses.

D) It does not address the technical aspects of Internet communication.

9. What will the future be like when everybody gets online?

A) People will be living in two different realities.

B) People will have equal access to information.

C) People don't have to travel to see the world.

D) People don't have to communicate face to face.

10. What does the passage say about the authors of *The New Digital Age*?

A) They leave many questions unanswered concerning the Internet.

B) They are optimistic about the future of the Internet revolution.

C) They have explored the unknown territories of the virtual world.

D) They don't take sides in analyzing the effects of the Internet.

Passage Three

Questions 11 to 15 are based on the following passage.

The endless debate about "work-life balance" often contains a hopeful footnote about stay-at-home dads. If American society and business won't make it easier on future female leaders who choose to have children, there is still the ray of hope that increasing numbers of full-time fathers will. But based on today's socioeconomic trends, this hope is, unfortunately, misguided.

It's true that the number of men who have left work to do their thing as full-time parents has doubled in a decade, but it's still very small: only 0.8% of married couples where the stay-at-home father was out of the labor force for a year. Even that percentage is likely inflated by men thrust into their caretaker role by a downsizing. This is simply not a large enough group to reduce the social stigma (污名) and force other adjustments necessary to supporting men in this decision, even if only for a relatively short time.

Even shorter times away from work for working fathers are already difficult. A study found that 85% of new fathers take some time off after the birth of a child—but for all but a few, it's a week or two at most. Meanwhile, the average for women who take leave is more than 10 weeks.

Such choices impact who moves up in the organization. While you're away, someone else is doing your work, making your sales, taking care of your customers. That can't help you at work. It can only hurt you. Women, of course, face the same issues of returning after a long absence. But with many more women than men choosing to leave the workforce entirely to raise families, returning from an extended parental leave doesn't raise as many eyebrows as it does for men.

Women would make more if they didn't break their earning trajectory (轨迹) by leaving the workforce, or if higher-paying professions were more family-friendly. In the foreseeable future, stay-at-home fathers may make all the difference for individual families, but their presence won't reduce the numbers of high-potential women who are forced to choose between family and career.

11. What gives women a ray of hope to achieve work-life balance?

A) More men taking an extended parental leave.

B) Peopled changing attitudes towards family.

C) More women entering business management.

D) The improvement of their socioeconomic status.

12. Why does the author say the hope for more full-time fathers is misguided?

A) Women are better at taking care of children.

B) Many men value work more than their family.

C) Their number is too small to make a difference.

D) Not many men have the chance to stay at home.

13. Why do few men take a long parental leave?

A) A long leave will have a negative impact on their career.

B) They just have too many responsibilities to fulfill at work.

C) The economic loss will be too much for their family to bear.

D) They are likely to get fired if absent from work for too long.

14. What is the most likely reaction to men returning from an extended parental leave?

A) Jealousy.

B) Surprise.

C) Admiration.

D) Sympathy.

15. What does the author say about high-potential women in the not-too-distant future?

A) They will benefit from the trend of more fathers staying at home.

B) They will find high-paying professions a bit more family-friendly.

C) They are unlikely to break their career trajectory to raise a family.

D) They will still face the difficult choice between career and children.

Passage Four

Questions 16 to 20 are based on the following passage.

Why do some people live to be older than others? You know the standard explanations: keeping a moderate diet, engaging in regular exercise, etc. But what effect does your personality have on your longevity (长寿)? Do some kinds of personalities lead to longer lives? A new study in the Journal of the American Geriatrics Society looked at this question by examining the personality characteristics of 246 children of people who had lived to be at least 100.

The study shows that those living the longest are more outgoing, more active and less neurotic (神经质的) than other people. Long-living women are also more likely to be sympathetic and co-operative than women with a normal life span. These findings are in agreement with what you would expect from the evolutionary theory: those who like to make friends and help others can gather enough resources to make it through tough times.

Interestingly, however, other characteristics that you might consider advantageous had no impact on whether study participants were likely to live longer. Those who were more self-disciplined, for instance, were no more likely to live to be very old. Also, being open to new ideas had no relationship to long life, which might explain all those bad-tempered old people who are fixed in their ways.

Whether you can successfully change your personality as an adult is the subject of a longstanding psychological debate. But the new paper suggests that if you want long life, you should strive to be as outgoing as possible.

Unfortunately, another recent study shows that your mother's personality may also help determine your longevity. That study looked at nearly 28,000 Norwegian mothers and found that those moms who were more anxious, depressed and angry were more likely to feed their kids unhealthy diets. Patterns of childhood eating can be hard to break when we're adults, which may mean that kids of depressed moms end up dying younger.

Personality isn't destiny (命运), and everyone knows that individuals can learn to change. But both studies show that long life isn't just a matter of your physical health but of, your mental health.

16. The aim of the study in the Journal of the American Geriatrics Society is _____.

A) to see whether people's personality affects their life span

B) to find out if one's lifestyle has any effect on their health

C) to investigate the role of exercise in living a long life

D) to examine all the factors contributing to longevity

17. What does the author imply about outgoing and sympathetic people?

A) They have a good understanding of evolution.

B) They are better at negotiating an agreement.

C) They generally appear more resourceful.

D) They are more likely to get over hardship.

18. What finding of the study might prove somewhat out of our expectation?

A) Easy-going people can also live a relatively long life.

B) Personality characteristics that prove advantageous actually vary with times.

C) Such personality characteristics as self-discipline have no effect on longevity.

D) Readiness to accept new ideas helps one enjoy longevity.

19. What does the recent study of Norwegian mothers show?

A) Children's personality characteristics are invariably determined by their mothers.

B) People with unhealthy eating habits are likely to die sooner.

C) Mothers' influence on children may last longer than fathers'.

D) Mothers' negative personality characteristics may affect their children's life span.

20. What can we learn from the findings of the two new studies?

A) Anxiety and depression more often than not cut short one's life span.

B) Longevity results from a combination of mental and physical health.

C) Personality plays a decisive role in how healthy one is.

D) Health is in large part related to one's lifestyle.

Part Two: Vocabulary and Structure (35%, 1 point each)

Directions: *there are 40 incomplete sentences in this part. For each sentence there are four choices marked completes the sentence. Then write the corresponding letter on the* **Answer Sheet**.

21. The conference _____ a full week by the time it ends.

A) must have lasted

B) will have lasted

C) would last

D) has lasted

22. _____ before we depart the day after tomorrow, we should have a wonderful dinner party.

A) Had they arrived

B) Would they arrive

C) Were they arriving

D) Were they to arrive

23. You see the lightning _____ it happens, but you hear the thunder later.

A) the instant

B) for an instant

C) on the instant

D) in an instant

24. It is important that enough money _____ to fund the project.

A) be collected

B) must be collected

C) was collected

D) can be collected

25. Great as Newton was, many of his ideas _____ today and are being modified by the work

of scientists of our time.

A) are to challenge

B) may be challenged

C) have been challenged

D) are challenging

26. He's watching TV? He's _____ to be cleaning his room.

A) known

B) supposed

C) regarded

D) considered

27. Studies show that the things that contribute most to a sense of happiness cannot be bought, _____ a good family life, friendship and work satisfaction.

A) as for

B) in view of

C) in case of

D) such as

28. The government is trying to do something to _____ better understanding between the two countries.

A) raise

B) promote

C) heighten

D) increase

29. The man in the corner confessed to _____ a lie to the manager of the company.

A) have told

B) be told

C) being told

D) having told

30. I don't think it advisable that Tom _____ to the job since he has no experience.

A) is assigned

B) will be assigned

C) be assigned

D) has been assigned

31. The car _____ halfway for no reason.

A) broke off

B) broke down

C) broke up

D) broke out

32. You have nothing to _____ by refusing to listen to our advice.

A) gain

B) grasp

C) seize

D) earn

33. One day I _____ a newspaper article about the retirement of an English professor at a nearby state college.

A) came across

B) came about

C) came after

D) came at

34. Since the matter was extremely _____, we dealt with it immediately.

A) tough

B) tense

C) urgent

D) instant

35. He hoped the firm would _____ him to the Paris branch.

A) exchange

B) transmit

C) transfer

D) remove

36. The shy girl felt _____ and uncomfortable when she could not answer her teacher's questions.

A) amazed

B) awkward

C) curious

D) amused

37. The patient's health failed to such an extent that he was put into _____ care.

A) tense

B) rigid

C) intensive

D) tight

38. We had to _____ a lot of noise when the children were at home.

A) go in for

B) hold on to

C) put up with

D) keep pace with

39. We are all for your proposal that the discussion _____ .

A) be put off

B) was put off

C) should put off

D) is to put off

40. These goods are _____ for export, though a few of them may be sold on the home market.

A) essentially

B) completely

C) necessarily

D) remarkably

41. Let's leave the question _____ for a moment.

A) off

B) out

C) down

D) aside

42. A large fish was slowly swimming through the water, its tail _____ back and forth like the pendulum of a clock.

A) swung

B) swinging

C) was swung

D) was swinging

43. The cells were designed to _____ sunshine to electricity to run a motor.

A) modify

B) alter

C) convert

D) exchange

44. The fire started on the first floor of the hospital, _____ are elderly and weak.

A) many of whose patients

B) many of which patients

C) many of its patients

D) many patients of whom

45. He was determined that none of his children would be _____ an education.

A) declined

B) canceled

C) denied

D) ceased

46. The jeweler assured Mr. White that the stone was a _____ diamond and not an imitation.

A) graceful

B) genuine

C) glittering

D) genius

47. In the southwestern part of the United States _____ built in the last century.

A) they are many abandoned mining towns

B) where there are many abandoned mining towns

C) are many abandoned mining towns

D) many abandoned mining towns are

48. As the clouds drifted away an even higher peak became _____ to the climbers.

A) visible

B) obvious

C) present

D) apparent

49. The remarkable gains in the general health of the population in the world have been due in large measure _____ the efforts of some great doctors.

A) for

B) with

C) by

D) to

50. He appeared in the court and supplied the facts _____ to the ease.

A) subject

B) relevant

C) attached

D) corresponding

51. A _____ exercise such as running is helpful to our health.

A) vigorous

B) cautious

C) precious

D) various

52. In sharp _____ to John, who is frank. Henry is too sophisticated.

A) conflict

B) contrast

C) comparison

D) contradiction

53. On a small farm in a dry climate one should not grow crops that need _____ space and a lot of water to ripen.

A) quantitative

B) significant

C) extensive

D) considerable

54. The doctor told the pupils that an _____ disease was one that could be passed from one person to another.

A) infectious

B) expanding

C) overwhelming

D) inherent

55. It would be surprising for _____ any objections to the proposal.

A) not to be

B) it not to be

C) there not to be

D) there to be not

Part Three: Cloze (10%, 1 point each)

Directions: *There are 10 blanks in the following passage. For each blank there are four choices marked A, B, C and D. You should choose the ONE that best fits into the passage. Then mark the corresponding letter on the **Answer Sheet**.*

Most Europeans want small cars. Many Americans (56) _____ large cars. As a result, European automakers produce a wide (57) _____ of economical, lightweight cars (58) _____ American automakers tend to bigger, heavier cars.

The price of gasoline has much to (59) _____ with this. Gasoline is expensive in Europe, so Europeans (60) _____ prefer cars that will go a long way on a small amount of fuel. Other (61) _____ also enter into the big or little car decision. Many European cities have very narrow, winding streets where a small car is more practical and easier to handle than a large one.

Some Americans like (62) _____ engines in their cars. They (63) _____ having roomy cars that are comfortable for large families and long (64) _____. They are prepared to pay higher (65) _____ costs to get these advantages.

56. A) operate   B) drive   C) ride   D) prefer
57. A) variety   B) series   C) specimen   D) sort
58. A) so   B) while   C) when   D) though
59. A) go   B) deal   C) do   D) say
60. A) mostly   B) instinctively C) willingly   D) naturally
61. A) reasons   B) ideas   C) opinions   D) attitudes
62. A) strong   B) durable   C) powerful   D) giant
63. A) recommend   B) appreciate   C) enjoy   D) suggest
64. A) holidays   B) tours   C) travels   D) trips
65. A) operating   B) maintaining   C) repairing   D) fueling

Part Four: Translation (15%, 3 points each)

Directions: *Read the following short passages carefully and translate the underlined sentences into Chinese. Please write your translation on **Answer Sheet***.

Having good friends is important for happiness. 66. <u>Friends provide support during difficult times.</u> 67. <u>Spending time with friends can bring joy and laughter.</u> 68. <u>Good friends help you feel less lonely and more connected.</u> 69. <u>It's important to communicate openly with your friends.</u> 70. <u>Building strong friendships can improve your overall well-being.</u>

第四部分　课文学习参考答案及课文译文

Unit 1　Fantastic Animals

Text A

Ⅰ. **Understanding the text**

1. Insects are, by far, the most common animals on our planet.

2. More than 1.5 million species of insects have been named.

3. Omnivorous.

4. They help keep pest populations (insects or weeds) at a tolerable level, which is part of the balance of nature.

5. Naturalists derive a great deal of satisfaction in watching ants work, bees pollinate, or dragonflies patrol.

Ⅱ. **Vocabulary and phrases**

1. combine　　2. diverse　　3. encounter　　4. survived　　5. primary
6. accumulation　7. fascinating　8. tolerable　　9. derives　　10. landscape

Ⅲ. **Translation**

1. 昆虫的体型、形状、颜色、生物学特征和生活史如此多样，这使得研究昆虫变得极其引人入胜。

2. 昆虫为许多水果、花卉和蔬菜授粉。

3. 这些昆虫在自然界中非常重要，因为它们有助于将害虫种群（昆虫或杂草）控制在可接受的水平。

4. 在某些文化中，昆虫被人们当作食物。因为它们富含蛋白质、维生素和矿物质。

5. 人类与昆虫共住同个世界，并从中获益良多。

Ⅳ. **Writing**（略）

Text B

Ⅰ. **Understanding the text**.

1. B　2. B　3. C　4. B　5. C

Ⅱ. Translation
1. 大象从年长大象的经验中学习。
2. 整个群体几乎所有事情都一起做。
3. 当一只大象去世时，其他大象常常会回到那个地方。
4. 大象之间有强烈的联系，可以持续许多年。
5. 一项研究发现，年长的大象在干旱期间帮助群体生存。

参考译文

Text A

昆虫的重要性

昆虫无处不在。迄今为止，它们是我们星球上最常见的动物。已命名的昆虫种类超过150万种，这是其他所有动物种类总和的三倍。昆虫的体型、形状、颜色、生物学特征和生活史如此多样，这使得研究昆虫变得极其引人入胜。

没有昆虫，我们的生活将大不相同。昆虫为许多水果、花卉和蔬菜授粉。如果没有昆虫的授粉服务，我们将无法享受到许多我们依赖的农产品，更不用提蜂蜜、丝绸和其他有用的昆虫制品了。

昆虫似乎能够食用几乎无限种类的食物。许多昆虫是杂食性的，这意味着它们可以吃各种食物，包括植物、死亡的动物、腐烂的有机物以及它们环境中几乎任何遇到的东西。还有一些昆虫在饮食方面是专家，这意味着它们可能只依赖一种特定的植物，甚至是一种特定植物的某个特定部分来生存。

许多昆虫是捕食性的或寄生性的，要么是对植物，要么是对其他昆虫或动物，包括人类。这些昆虫在自然界中非常重要，因为它们有助于将害虫种群（昆虫或杂草）控制在可接受的水平。我们称之为大自然的平衡。捕食性和寄生性昆虫在攻击我们认为有害的其他动物或植物时非常有价值。

昆虫作为初级或次级分解者非常重要。如果没有昆虫帮助分解和处理废物，死亡的动物和植物将在我们的环境中堆积，环境将变得非常杂乱无章。

昆虫在食物网中也扮演着重要的角色。它们是许多鸟类和动物的唯一食物来源。在某些文化中，昆虫被人们当作食物。因为它们富含蛋白质、维生素和矿物质。

而且，昆虫让我们的世界变得更加有趣。自然学家在观察蚂蚁工作、蜜蜂授粉或蜻蜓捕猎中会获得极大的满足感。你能想象如果没有蝴蝶或萤火虫为风景增添趣味，生活会变得多么乏味吗？人类与昆虫共住同个世界，并从中获益良多。

Text B

深层象群文化

大象不仅有惊人的身体特征，还有丰富的文化历史。大象的历史通过它们的习俗和社会行为传承下来，年轻的大象学习、记住并与它们的群体分享这些行为。这些行为对它们的生存和生活的安宁非常重要。

大象学习一部分是因为它们独特的社会结构。大象生活在紧密的群体中，由多代大象组成，由年长的雌性领导，称为母象。年轻的大象观察并模仿年长的大象，从它们的经验中学习。整个群体几乎一起做所有事情，比如寻找食物、吃东西和照顾彼此的小象。这些活动建立的强烈的关系，可以持续许多年，甚至几十年。

由于这些强烈的联系，大象似乎有感情，就像人类一样。它们会在有一只大象去世时表现出悲伤。当一只大象去世时，其他大象常常会回到它去世的地方。这种行为似乎是它们哀悼的一部分。它们可能会闻和触摸尸体，并用树叶覆盖那个地方。一项2020年的研究发现，"大象对死亡的个体表现出兴趣，不管它们以前的关系如何。"这表明大象具有较高的意识和理解能力。

在许多语言中有一句话："大象永远不会忘记事情。"实际上，大象的良好记忆对某些群体的生存非常重要。在大克鲁格国家公园的一项研究中发现，在2016年严重干旱期间，由经历过干旱的年长雌性大象领导的群体存活率更高。

因此，认为自己很幸运，能与这些庞大而美妙的动物分享这个星球。

Unit 2　Artificial Intelligence

Text A

Ⅰ. Understanding the text

1. AI-powered virtual assistants can manage our calendars, schedule appointments, set reminders, and organize our to-do lists.

2. By managing our calendars and setting reminders.

3. They can monitor health and track activity.

4. Photo editing applications use AI algorithms to enhance images. Music composition tools can generate melodies based on users' input.

5. It's important to use AI responsibly, ensuring it benefits society as a whole.

Ⅱ. Vocabulary and phrases

1. optimize　　2. virtual　　3. smoother　　4. generate　　5. Wearable
6. contribute　　7. preferences　　8. adapt　　9. efficient　　10. instant

Ⅲ. Translation

1. 配备人工智能的可穿戴设备可以监测我们的健康状况，跟踪我们的活动情况，甚至预测潜在问题。

2. 远程医疗平台利用人工智能提供远程医生咨询服务，让我们无需亲自到诊所就能获得医疗帮助。

3. 电子邮件应用程序使用人工智能对我们的消息进行分类，并对收件箱进行优先级排序。

4. 照片编辑应用程序利用人工智能算法增强图像，并提出符合我们审美偏好的编辑建议。

5. 随着人工智能的不断进步，它改善我们日常生活的潜力也在不断增长。

Ⅳ. Writing（略）

Text B

Ⅰ. Understanding the text.

1. The mobile phone's Face ID system tracks changes in the user's appearance over time and updates the authentication model accordingly.

2. Celia leverages natural language processing and machine learning to interpret the user's spoken commands.

3. Xiaomi SU7 car's self-driving system can handle situations it has encountered before, but struggles with rare or unexpected events.

4. The medical field is investing in AI research and applications, from scan analysis to precision surgery.

5. AI is transforming the hiring process, with applicants using AI to craft personalized cover letters, and companies employing AI algorithms to screen and score candidates.

Ⅱ. **Translation**

1. 人工智能已经深深融入我们的日常生活。
2. 这个人工智能系统会随着时间的推移跟踪你的外表变化，并相应地更新其身份验证模型。
3. 语音助手小艺（Celia）利用自然语言处理和机器学习来解释你的语音命令。
4. 从扫描分析到精准手术，医疗领域正在大力投资人工智能的研究和应用。
5. 人工智能的影响无处不在，重塑着我们日常生活的方方面面。

参考译文

Text A

人工智能对我们日常生活的影响

在当今快节奏的世界中，技术，尤其是人工智能已经成为我们日常生活的重要组成部分。从我们醒来到躺下休息的那一刻，人工智能都在幕后默默地工作，让我们的日常体验更顺畅、更智能、更愉快。

人工智能技术可以简化我们的日常任务，使我们的日常工作更加高效和方便。人工智能驱动的虚拟助手可以管理我们的日历、安排约会、设置提醒和组织我们的待办事项列表。凭借自然语言处理和机器学习功能，这些助手可以了解我们的偏好并适应我们的需求，确保我们轻松完成任务。

在医疗保健领域，人工智能正在发挥巨大作用。配备人工智能的可穿戴设备可以监测我们的健康状况，跟踪我们的活动情况，甚至预测潜在问题。远程医疗平台利用人工智能提供远程医生咨询服务，让我们无需亲自到诊所就能获得医疗帮助。

人工智能还可以改善沟通。电子邮件应用程序使用人工智能对我们的消息进行分类，并对收件箱进行优先级排序。网站和社交媒体平台上的聊天机器人提供即时客户支持，及时回答问题并解决问题。人工智能驱动的语言翻译工具使我们能够弥合人与人之间的沟通差距，无论使用何种语言。

此外，人工智能正在为创造性工作做出贡献。照片编辑应用程序利用人工智能算法增强图像，并提出符合我们审美偏好的编辑建议。音乐创作工具可以根据我们的输入生成旋律，激发音乐家和业余爱好者的灵感，去探索新的艺术领域。这些创新使个人能够以人工智能为合作伙伴，创造性地表达自己。

随着人工智能的不断进步，它改善我们日常生活的潜力也在不断增长。配备人工智能驱动系统的智能家居可以调节照明、温度和安全性。自动驾驶汽车有望实现更安全、更高效的通勤。预测分析可以优化供应链。

人工智能融入我们的日常生活不仅仅是一种趋势，也是我们与技术互动方式的一个重大变化。通过使任务更容易、个性化体验、彻底改变医疗保健、增强沟通以及激发创造力，人工智能正在为更方便、高效和量身定制的生活方式打开大门。当我们拥抱人工智能的变革力量时，负责任地使用它，确保它造福整个社会非常重要。

Text B

人工智能生活中的一天

人工智能（AI）已经深深融入我们的日常生活。从我们醒来时使用的 iPhone，到我们开车上班的电动汽车，再到我们工作的医院，人工智能都在发挥作用。

早上 7 点，你瞥了一眼你的手机，它使用人脸识别解锁。这个人工智能系统会随着时间的推移跟踪你的外表变化，并相应地更新其身份验证模型。手机的相机应用程序还利用计算机视觉来识别人和物体，对图像进行分类。语音助手 Celia 利用自然语言处理和机器学习来解释你的语音命令。

早上 7 点 40 分，你让 Celia 播放音乐。Celia 将你的录音发送到亚马逊的服务器，语音识别软件将音频转换为文本。然后，语言处理算法会提取含义，并将响应发送回你的设备。Celia 的学习过程包括对样本请求进行人工审查，以不断提高其能力。

上午 8 点 10 分，你开着小米 SU7 去上班。汽车的 AI 系统从八个摄像头收集数据，识别障碍物、车道、十字路口和交通信号灯，并做出适当的操作。然而，这些自动驾驶汽车仅限于处理它们以前遇到的情况，难以应对罕见或意外的事件。

上午 9 点到达医院后，你会看到从扫描分析到精准手术，医疗领域正在大力投资人工智能的研究和应用。肺部健康筛查项目使用基于人工智能的计算机辅助检测来协助识别肺结节，并由医生进行最终诊断。

午休时间，你帮助女儿完善她的求职信。人工智能正在改变招聘流程，求职者使用 AI 工具制作个性化的求职信，公司采用人工智能算法对候选人进行筛选和评分。

人工智能的影响无处不在，重塑着我们日常生活的方方面面。尽管这项技术仍然存在局限性，但人工智能已经成为我们生活、工作和互动中不可或缺的一部分。

Unit 3 Sports and Fitness

Text A

Ⅰ. Understanding the text

1. Exercising in the morning can lead to increased physical activity throughout the day, less distraction from food, and better sleep.

2. According to the 2010 study, the body's ability to perform peaks in the afternoon.

3. In the afternoon and evening, the heart rate and blood pressure are lowest, which can reduce the chance of injury while improving performance.

4. The 2022 study found that for women, exercising in the morning is better for reducing blood pressure, while for men, exercising in the evening is better for improving heart health.

5. The ultimate conclusion is that the best time to exercise is whatever time is best for you.

Ⅱ. Vocabulary and phrases

1. maximize   2. Compared to   3. exact   4. peak   5. benefits
6. participant   7. pressure   8. physical   9. distractions   10. stick

Ⅲ. Translation

1. 与一天中的晚些时候相比，我们中的许多人早上拥有更多的空闲时间，因此我们可能更容易坚持早上的锻炼习惯。

2. 早餐前空腹锻炼也可以燃烧更多的脂肪并提高代谢，这意味着你一整天都会继续消耗卡路里。

3. 此外，在下午和晚上，你的反应速度最快，心率和血压最低，这可以降低受伤的概率，同时提高表现。

4. 对于想要降低血压的女性来说，早上锻炼更有益。

5. 然而，该研究的总体发现是，无论何时，不同性别的人都可以从锻炼中获得明显的好处。

Ⅳ. Writing（略）

Text B

Ⅰ. Understanding the text.

1. According to the research, watching sports events can increase the risk of cardiovascular incidents due to the emotional stress.

2. The study found that sports spectators feel less lonely and have higher life satisfaction compared to non-viewers, as watching live sports provides social interaction and a sense of belonging.

3. Even watching sports on TV/online can have positive effects, as older adults who watched

sports were less likely to have depressive symptoms, possibly due to the social networks gained.

4. The research indicates that sports spectators tend to have richer social networks than non-spectators.

5. Overall, watching sports, whether live or remotely, can bring a sense of camaraderie and may reduce loneliness and depression, providing health benefits beyond just physical activity.

Ⅱ. Translation

1. 如果你是个体育迷，你可能熟悉作为体育观众所经历的情绪过山车。

2. 研究结果表明，观看现场体育赛事的人比不观看的人幸福感更强。

3. 根据该研究，观看各种类型的现场体育赛事都为社交互动提供了许多机会，这有助于培养群体认同感和归属感。

4. 这项研究的作者认为，通过观看体育赛事而培养的社交联系和互动，可能有助于降低出现抑郁症状的风险。

5. 看来，体育带来的健康益处不仅限于通过参与运动获得的身体活动，我们也能通过社交纽带获得总体幸福感的提升。

参考译文

Text A

是否有最佳的锻炼时间？

我们的生活已经很忙碌了，找到锻炼的时间可能会感觉像是增加了另一项待办事项。那么，是否存在"最佳锻炼时间"呢？在某些时间锻炼是否能更好地帮助我们实现健身目标？答案是"是的"，但要比你想象的简单得多——不管你是谁，或者喜欢什么时候锻炼。

早上锻炼确实有明显的好处。与一天中的晚些时候相比，我们中的许多人早上拥有更多的空闲时间，因此我们可能更容易坚持早上的锻炼习惯。一项发表在《运动医学与科学》上的研究发现，参与者在早上锻炼，全天的身体活动都有所增加，对食物的注意力也更少，睡眠质量也更好。早餐前空腹锻炼也可以燃烧更多的脂肪并提高代谢，这意味着你一整天都会继续消耗卡路里。

所以，对于早起的人来说，这是个好消息。但如果你不是一个早起的人呢？下午或晚上锻炼也有好处，只是不同的好处。例如，根据2010年《斯堪的纳维亚运动医学和科学杂志》的一项研究，你的身体在下午的表现能力达到峰值。此外，在下午和晚上，你的反应速度最快，心率和血压最低，这可以降低受伤的概率，同时提高表现。

但是，这是否会因性别的不同而改变？毕竟，我们的身体是不同的，最佳锻炼时间也可能不同。2022年的一项研究就探讨了这个问题，结果显示存在一些差异。对于想要降低血压的女性来说，早上锻炼更有益。相反，对于想要改善心脏健康的男性来说，晚上似乎是更好的时间。然而，该研究的总体发现是，无论何时，不同性别的人都可以从锻炼中获得明显的好处。

那么，什么时间最佳呢？答案似乎是：对你来说最合适的时间！

Text B

观看体育运动对你的幸福感有好处吗？

如果你是个体育迷，你可能熟悉作为体育观众所经历的情绪过山车。无论你是身在沸腾的体育场看现场比赛，还是在家里电视前观看，当你与喜欢的球队或运动员一起欢庆或哀悼时，很容易被情感的起伏所吸引。事实上，一项来自克罗地亚的研究还显示，在足球比赛期间经历的情绪压力可能会增加心血管事件的风险。然而，问题仍然存在——观看体育运动是否也会对人的幸福感产生积极影响？

研究结果表明，观看现场体育赛事的人比不观看的人幸福感更强。英国安格利亚鲁斯金大学进行的一项研究发现，体育观众感到孤独感更低，生活满意度更高。根据该研究，观看各种类型的现场体育赛事都为社交互动提供了许多机会，这有助于培养群体认同感和归属感。这种社交参与最终减少了孤独感，提高了整体幸福感。

但是，如果出于某种原因你不太喜欢去现场观看，也不用担心！根据2021年的一项研究，在电视或网上观看体育比赛也可能产生积极影响。研究发现，观看体育运动的老年人比不观看的人更不容易出现抑郁症状。此外，这项研究还发现，体育观众往往拥有比非观众更广泛的社交网络。这项研究的作者认为，通过观看体育赛事而培养的社交联系和互动，可能有助于降低出现抑郁症状的风险。

所以，在现场体育赛事中的欢呼声，或者与朋友们轻松讨论喜欢的球队，都可以带来一种团结感，并减少孤独和抑郁。看来，体育带来的健康益处不仅限于通过参与运动获得的身体活动，我们也能通过社交纽带获得总体幸福感的提升。

Unit 4　Healthy Habits

Text A

Ⅰ. Understanding the text

1. Nearly 72% of adults in the UK had a houseplant in their home.

2. According to the passage, more young people are living in flats without a garden, which makes houseplants an appealing option.

3. Buying houseplants that are shipped from far-away locations can be harmful to the environment due to the carbon footprint and negative impact.

4. Others are worried about the plastic pots they are in and the type of peat that some of them are grown in.

5. To address the concerns about the environmental impact of buying houseplants that are shipped from overseas.

Ⅱ. Vocabulary and phrases

1. surround　　2. purchasing　　3. commitment　　4. boost　　5. quality

6. concerns　　7. multiple　　8. atmosphere　　9. plastic　　10. brighten

Ⅲ. Translation

1. 这是一个我们被自己的财物和舒适享受所包围的地方。
2. 但是，这些"活的"家庭添置物对我们和环境有益吗？
3. 从遥远的地方购买室内植物并运输到家中，会对环境造成伤害。
4. 植物运输的距离越远，无论是空运、海运还是陆运，其碳足迹和负面影响就越大。
5. 送货上门的环境影响要小于多次开车去园艺中心。

Ⅳ. Writing（略）

Text B

Ⅰ. Understanding the text.

1. The passage mentions working at a desk, sitting motionless in a car/bus/train, and lounging on the sofa watching TV as common sedentary activities.

2. The study showed that bus drivers, who spent many hours sitting, were twice as likely to have heart attacks than the more active ticket collectors.

3. One possible solution is for desk workers to use standing desks and spend at least part of their day on their feet.

4. Another study suggested that by standing for three or four hours a day over the period of a year, people would burn as many calories as if they had run ten marathons.

5. The experts recommend that if people do use standing desks, they should gradually increase the amount of time they spend on their feet.

Ⅱ. Translation

1. 无论是在桌前工作、一动不动地坐在汽车、公共汽车或火车上,还是在沙发上看电视,我们的生活方式比父母和祖父母更加久坐。

2. 结果发现,长时间坐在方向盘上的司机比更活跃的售票员更容易心脏病发作,概率是后者的两倍。

3. 事实上,长时间坐着已经与多种健康问题有关,即使是那些平时经常锻炼的人。

4. 一项小型研究显示,午餐后站立3个小时的办公室员工,血糖水平的升幅要小得多。

5. 他们还指出,有许多替代久坐的方式,它们的影响可能不尽相同:比如步行就能消耗远多于站立的热量。

参考译文

Text A

室内植物:利弊如何?

家就是家,这是一个我们被自己的财物和舒适享受所包围的地方。我们购买各种物品来给家添加个人特色,营造一种氛围。我们越来越多地购买室内植物。但是,这些"活的"家庭添置物对我们和环境有益吗?

室内植物,也称为盆栽植物,在社交媒体上很受欢迎;它们能增添自然气息,而且无需太多成本就能让房间更加明亮。一项研究发现,近72%的成年人家里有室内植物,这一比例在16~24岁的年轻人中更是高达80%。五分之一的主人还表示,他们使用室内植物来提高自己的健康和幸福感。去年植物销量较前一年有所上升。

似乎千禧一代正在推动室内植物销售的增长。根据研究,越来越多的年轻人居住在没有花园的公寓里。24岁的黛西·黑尔说:"能照顾一些东西,但又不需要太多承诺,这对我的生活方式来说是理想的。"

室内植物有多种类型,从吊篮到仙人掌和蕨类植物应有尽有。它们照顾起来很容易,而且也有一些未经证实的说法称,它们可以改善家中的空气质量。但不管它们的好处如何,现在也有人担心它们可能并不太环保。一些植物是在网上购买并从海外运送过来的。从遥远的地方购买室内植物并运输到家中,会对环境造成伤害。植物运输的距离越远,无论是空运、海运还是陆运,其碳足迹和负面影响就越大。

但是,植物学家詹姆斯·王认为送货上门的环境影响要小于多次开车去园艺中心。尽管他并不太担心环境影响,但其他人担心它们所使用的塑料盆和一些使用泥炭培育的类型。然而,如果我们想把一些自然的绿色引入家中,采取可持续的购买方式可能是最好的办法。

Text B

久坐的危害

你知道吗，很多成年人一天坐下来超过 9 个小时——也许你就是其中之一！无论是在桌前工作、一动不动地坐在汽车、公共汽车或火车上，还是在沙发上看电视，我们的生活方式比父母和祖父母更加久坐。这引出了一个问题，这对我们的身体有什么影响？

结果并不乐观。20 世纪 50 年代的一项研究将公交车司机与售票员进行了比较，结果发现，长时间坐在方向盘上的司机比更活跃的售票员更容易心脏病发作，概率是后者的两倍。事实上，长时间坐着已经与多种健康问题有关，即使是那些平时经常锻炼的人。如果你整天坐着，消耗的热量要远远少于从事更多活动的人。有证据表明，这会降低你的代谢率，让你的身体更难控制血糖水平，从而增加患糖尿病的风险。

解决这个问题的一个办法是让办公桌工作的人使用站立式办公桌，每天至少有一部分时间站着工作。一项小型研究显示，午餐后站立 3 个小时的办公室员工，血糖水平的升幅要小得多，另一项研究也表明，每天站立 3~4 个小时，一年下来消耗的卡路里，相当于跑了 10 个马拉松。

不过，也有专家对这一数据提出质疑，指出整天站立也可能产生负面影响，如腿部或背部疼痛。他们建议，如果使用站立式办公桌，应该逐步增加站立的时间。他们还指出，有许多替代久坐的方式，它们的影响可能不尽相同：比如步行就能消耗远多于站立的热量。

Unit 5　Work and Life

Text A

Ⅰ. Understanding the text

1. An ice cream taster in England is responsible for tasting different flavors of ice cream and providing feedback on the flavors and textures to help companies create new recipes or improve existing ones.

2. Dialect coaches play a crucial role in helping actors master regional accents and speech patterns to ensure the characters they portray on stage or screen are authentic.

3. Penguin keepers in Antarctica must be willing to adapt to the challenges of living and working in the harsh, remote, and difficult Antarctic environment.

4. The work of a translator for endangered languages contributes to language preservation by documenting and preserving languages that are at risk of disappearing, ensuring that the rich cultural heritage they represent is not lost.

5. The role of a professional mourner in Japan highlights the importance of honoring and preserving cultural rituals related to grief and mourning.

Ⅱ. Vocabulary and phrases

1. offers　　2. requires　　3. feedback　　4. harsh　　5. challenges
6. remote　　7. preserve　　8. specific　　9. observe　　10. explore

Ⅲ. Translation

1. 这份工作需要品尝各种口味的冰淇淋，并就口味和质地给予反馈。

2. 他们必须对野生动物保护有浓厚兴趣，并愿意适应在这个偏远困难的地区生活和工作的挑战。

3. 对于那些对语言保护感兴趣的人来说，濒危语言翻译员的工作提供了一个独特的机会来产生持久的影响。

4. 这些人受雇参加葬礼，代表悲伤的家人表达悲痛和哀悼。

5. 这五种独特而引人入胜的职业只是世界各地众多非凡工作机会的一小部分。

Ⅳ. Writing（略）

Text B

Ⅰ. Understanding the text.

1. The evolution of video games has given rise to the career path of the professional gamer.

2. Professional gamers spend hours every day working out hacks to save time or improve their chances of winning.

3. Exercising and stretching is vital for professional gamers to avoid injuries to their backs and wrists and to prevent eye fatigue from spending long hours staring at monitors.

4. According to experts, some of the psychological impacts that professional gamers need to be careful with are regulating emotions, dealing with pressure and big crowds, and overcoming injury.

5. The transition from amateur to pro is paved with countless hours of practice, perseverance, and the willingness to adapt to the unique demands of the rapidly growing e-sports industry.

Ⅱ. Translation

1. 在游戏发展的早期，热衷于电子游戏的人通常会在幕后担任开发者、测试员或程序员的工作。

2. 虽然选择最佳装备很重要，比如合适的手柄或键盘，但大多数职业选手每天都要花数小时寻找节省时间或提高获胜机会的技巧。

3. 情绪调节、应对压力和大型观众群、克服伤病等都是共同因素。

4. 因此，尽管职业游戏玩家的生活可能看起来光鲜亮丽且无忧无虑，但实际上这是一个需要坚定奉献和纪律的追求。

5. 从业余选手到职业选手的转变，需要无数小时的练习、毅力和适应这个快速发展行业独特需求的意愿。

参考译文
Text A

世界各地有趣的工作

你有没有想过从事一些不太多人做过的工作？世界各地存在许多独特而非凡的工作，它们提供了不同种类的工作经验，让你可以以与大多数其他工作不同的方式探索自己的创造力、技能和兴趣。以下是其中五种：

英国的冰淇淋品尝师

你喜欢冰淇淋吗？如果喜欢，你可以成为英国的冰淇淋品尝师。这份工作需要品尝各种口味的冰淇淋，并就口味和质地给予反馈。这有助于公司创造新配方或改进现有配方。冰淇淋品尝师必须能够清楚地描述他们的品尝体验。

南极洲的企鹅饲养员

企鹅饲养员负责照顾南极恶劣环境中的企鹅群落。他们必须对野生动物保护有浓厚兴趣，并愿意适应在这个偏远困难的地区生活和工作的挑战。企鹅饲养员观察企鹅的行为，确保它们的安全和福祉，这有助于保护脆弱的南极生态系统。

英国的方言教练

在表演艺术中，方言教练在帮助演员掌握地区口音和语言模式方面发挥了关键作用。这确保他们在舞台或银幕上塑造的角色是真实可信的。方言教练必须深入了解语言的微妙差异，并有能力有效地向演员传授这些细微差异。

濒危语言的翻译员

对于那些对语言保护感兴趣的人来说，濒危语言翻译员的工作提供了一个独特的机会来产生持久的影响。这些翻译员致力于记录和保护那些面临消失风险的语言，确保它们所代表的丰富文化遗产不会丢失。这个角色需要精通濒危语言，并深入了解塑造该语言的历史和文化背景。

日本的职业哀悼者

在日本，有一个独特的职业叫作"职业哀悼者"。这些人受雇参加葬礼，代表悲伤的家人表达悲痛和哀悼。职业哀悼者必须具备情商，能够传达真挚动人的悲痛，并有能力根据死者的特定文化和宗教传统调整自己的表演。这个角色突出了尊重和保留文化仪式的重要性。

这五种独特而引人入胜的职业只是世界各地众多非凡工作机会的一小部分。通过拥抱非常规的道路，个人可以开启一个独特体验、个人成长的世界，并有机会在所选领域产生深远影响。

Text B

职业游戏玩家的生活

从20世纪70年代开始，电子游戏发展了很多，变得更加沉浸式。但不仅仅是图形和游戏机制发生了变化。这种演变也催生了一种新的职业道路：职业游戏玩家。

在游戏发展的早期，热衷于电子游戏的人通常会在幕后担任开发者、测试员或程序员的工作。虽然竞技性游戏活动是存在的，但它们更多被视为爱好，而非可行的职业选择。然而，2000年后期直播平台的兴起为游戏玩家开启了成为名人的道路。

如今，随着电子竞技已成为游戏不可或缺的一部分，职业游戏玩家的生活是什么样的？根据许多职业选手的说法，关键在于练习，这与许多传统体育项目一样。虽然选择最佳装备很重要，比如合适的手柄或键盘，但大多数职业选手每天都要花数小时寻找节省时间或提高获胜机会的技巧。他们不仅需要在玩游戏时保持积极活跃，在现实生活中也是如此。锻炼和拉伸对于预防背部和手腕受伤以及通过定期休息屏幕来防止眼睛疲劳都至关重要。

但游戏玩家需要小心的不仅仅是身体方面。据菲尔·伯奇博士等专家称，尽管电子竞技和传统体育的身体需求非常不同，但其心理影响可能类似：情绪调节、应对压力和大型观众群、克服伤病等都是共同因素。

因此，尽管职业游戏玩家的生活可能看起来光鲜亮丽且无忧无虑，但实际上这是一个需要坚定奉献和纪律的追求。从业余选手到职业选手的转变，需要无数小时的练习、毅力和适应这个快速发展行业独特需求的意愿。

Unit 6　Starting a Business

Text A

Ⅰ. Understanding the text

1. The passage suggests that some young adults may feel that starting a business is something they will do when they are older and have more experience.

2. The most important quality an entrepreneur needs is enthusiasm and passion for their work.

3. Young entrepreneurs may worry about having less experience and knowledge compared to their older employees.

4. In addition to ideas, entrepreneurs also need financial backing and expert guidance to start a new business.

5. The passage advises that if you don't have the desire to start a business and make your fortune, you should keep on studying—an education is priceless.

Ⅱ. Vocabulary and phrases

1. minimum   2. spotted   3. desire   4. priceless   5. proving

6. admitted   7. drawback   8. executive 9. enthusiasm 10. intellect

Ⅲ. Translation

1. 还有很多其他年轻企业家的例子，他们取得了巨大成功，证明要成为顶级老板并没有最低年龄限制。

2. 你需要培养敏捷的智力和扎实的商业技能。

3. 年轻人在商业中确实也面临一些缺点；你可能会担心自己没有什么可以贡献的，而且为你工作的人往往更老练和睿智。

4. 你可能认为创办一家新的初创公司说起来容易做起来难。

5. 除了想法，你还需要资金支持和专业指导。

Ⅳ. Writing（略）

Text B

Ⅰ. Understanding the text

1. A side hustle is a second job or additional business activity that someone undertakes alongside their main employment.

2. The average side hustler makes about 20% of their income through their second job.

3. Research has found that almost three-quarters of millennials are taking on side hustles to follow a passion or explore a new challenge, not just for money and security.

4. Mobile apps from companies like Meituan, Xianyu, Pinduoduo and Zhihu allow people to

easily take on a variety of temporary, flexible side jobs from their phones.

5. A side hustle can be a good way to test out a potential new career path or pursue a passion, without fully giving up the stability of a day job.

Ⅱ. **Translation**

1. 但它也会带来好处，比如固定的薪资，有时还有工作满足感。

2. 对于一些人来说，拥有两份工作是必需的，这是一种维持生计和获得额外收入的方式。

3. 这些人往往是富有创业精神的年轻人，他们希望在主要收入来源之外，从事自己的项目。

4. 移动应用程序也有助于更具商业头脑的副业者。

5. 当然，拥有一个副业意味着你是自主创业，或者是自由职业者。这可以让你更灵活地安排工作时间，但也可能有风险。

参考译文

Text A

年轻商务人

你有商业头脑吗？你是否一直在寻找下一个大点子？也许和我一样，你可能觉得创办一家新公司是成熟后的事，当你有更多经验时才会去做。但并非总是如此。

虽然我们中的一些人可能觉得成年初期是犹豫找到自己在这个世界的位置、睡到很晚和努力玩乐的时期，但另一些人已经在通往巨大商业成功的道路上了。以微软创始人比尔·盖茨为例，他在美国哈佛大学时就创办了自己的公司。还有很多其他年轻企业家的例子，他们取得了巨大成功，证明要成为顶级老板并没有最低年龄限制。

但要成为下一个商业巨头需要付出努力。你需要培养敏捷的智力和扎实的商业技能。但最重要的是，你必须对工作充满热情和激情。开办新企业伴随着一定风险，但如果你能发现下一个大点子，那么尝试一下可能是值得的。杰西卡·罗斯经营一家珠宝制作公司，她承认"当我刚开始的时候，我完全没有任何商业培训……但有一天我醒来，突然觉得我真的很想成为一名珠宝设计师。"她最终成了一名成功的年轻企业家。

年轻人在商业中确实也面临一些缺点；你可能会担心自己没有什么可以贡献的，而且为你工作的人往往更老练和睿智。这就是年轻的英国企业家萨克拉尼所遇到的问题。他在读化学专业的时候就开始了自己的第三家企业。他说"现在我有了两位额外的董事，他们都有白发"但刚开始的时候，他能感觉到他们"在心里在想，'我面前坐的是一个孩子。'"

你可能认为创办一家新的初创公司说起来容易做起来难。除了想法，你还需要资金支持和专业指导。但是如果你在大学里刻苦学习，不想进入商界创造财富，那就继续学习吧——教育是无价的！

Text B

副业

你有工作吗？如果有，你就会知道工作的世界并非一帆风顺——工作时间长、任务烦琐、压力大。但它也会带来好处，比如固定的薪资，有时还有工作满足感。也许这就是为什么越来越多的人现在开始从事副业——第二份工作的另一个名字。

对于一些人来说，拥有两份工作是必需的，这是一种维持生计和获得额外收入的方式。但现在似乎有更多的人想把自己的技能和激情付诸实践来赚钱。这些人往往是富有创业精神的年轻人，他们希望在主要收入来源之外，从事自己的项目。

根据亨利商学院的数据，大约四分之一的工人经营着至少一个副业，其中一半是在过去两年内开始的。25 至 34 岁的人最有可能参与其中，37% 的人被认为经营着某种副业。据计算，普通副业者通过第二份工作赚取约 20% 的收入。

但有趣的是，许多千禧一代不仅仅是为了金钱和安全感而从事新的工作。研究发现，近四分之三的人是出于追求热情或探索新的挑战。周小白一部分时间为电信公司工作来付账单，但剩下的时间都用在发展她的手工制作公司。她说全职工作"在财务上目前还不值得，但它滋养了我的创造灵魂，让我感到快乐"。

移动应用程序也有助于更具商业头脑的副业者。美团、咸鱼、拼多多、知乎等点对点公司允许用户从手机上完成从零工到出租房屋和停车位的各种工作。

当然，拥有一个副业意味着你是自主创业，或者是自由职业者。这可以让你更灵活地安排工作时间，但也可能有风险。有时你可能会签订零工时合同，并且可能无法获得足够的工作。或者最初的激情工作最终变成了负担。然而，这可能是尝试新的职业或追求热情又不放弃日常工作的最佳方式。

Unit 7　Leisure Activities

Text A

Ⅰ. **Understanding the text**

1. The three options are a five-star hotel, a self-catering apartment, or sleeping under canvas (camping).

2. The passage states that experts say a few peaceful nights in the middle of nowhere might be a good way to unwind and improve sleep patterns and well-being.

3. More people have opted for a staycation within the UK, which has caused a surge in demand for camping gear.

4. Additional items like inflatable mattresses and pillows, powerful torches and lamps, and a better selection of easy-to-cook food can help guarantee a comfortable and enjoyable camping expedition.

5. For the adventurous, wild camping involves being "armed with just some food and a sleeping bag" and being "free from rules, away from other people".

Ⅱ. **Vocabulary and phrases**

1. facility　　2. accessory　　3. hectic　　4. adventurous　　5. notification

6. budget　　7. luxurious　　8. opted　　9. guarantee　　10. cater

Ⅲ. **Translation**

1. 只需拿上帐篷和一些额外的配件，就可以很容易地前往乡村，在星空下度过一两个晚上。

2. 受专家的鼓励，许多露营者都抛开了现代繁忙的生活，专家认为在荒野中度过几个宁静的夜晚可能是放松和改善睡眠模式及身心健康的好方法。

3. 对于喜欢冒险的人来说，野营是从现实中逃离的最终方式。

4. 只带着一些食物和睡袋，你就可以摆脱规则，远离他人，体验返璞归真的体验。

5. 最近，由于更多人选择在英国国内度假，露营装备的销量也有所飙升。

Ⅳ. **Writing**（略）

Text B

Ⅰ. **Understanding the text**.

1. The physical effort required in singing, such as deep breathing, vocal cord control, and mouth/body movement, as well as the release of endorphins or "happy hormones".

2. Precisely hitting each note involves breathing control and the use of the diaphragm, which can increase oxygen intake and lung capacity.

3. It shows that a large number of people in Britain have taken up group singing as a regular activity.

4. Choral singing enhances feelings of trust and bonding among a group, which can help with depression and loneliness.

5. Yes, because the benefits of singing are plentiful, even if one occasionally forgets the lyrics or sounds a bit off-key.

Ⅱ. **Translation**

1. 无论你是卡拉OK巨星还是只在私密的淋浴间中享受歌唱的人，研究表明唱歌都能带来身心健康的好处。

2. 精准地唱出每个音符需要呼吸控制和利用肺活门。这可以增加氧气摄入量和肺活量。

3. 据估计，现在英国已经有220多万人定期参加合唱团。

4. 合唱能增强群体间的信任感和凝聚力，有助于缓解抑郁和孤独。

5. 是的，你偶尔会忘词或音准有些偏离，但请记住，唱歌的好处是多方面的。

参考译文

Text A

为什么户外露营这么有趣？

当你去度假时，你喜欢住在什么地方？你喜欢五星级酒店的奢华，自助公寓的便利，还是更喜欢在帐篷下自由入眠？如果你还没有尝试过后者，也许你应该加入越来越多正在享受露营简单乐趣的人。

只需拿上帐篷和一些额外的配件，就可以很容易地前往乡村，在星空下度过一两个晚上。受专家的鼓励，许多露营者都抛开了现代繁忙的生活，专家认为在荒野中度过几个宁静的夜晚可能是放松和改善睡眠模式及身心健康的好方法。这当然也是一种低成本的假期选择。

对于喜欢冒险的人来说，野营是从现实中逃离的最终方式。只带着一些食物和睡袋，你就可以摆脱规则，远离他人，体验返璞归真的体验。一位野营者菲比·史密斯说："当其他人都回家后，你独自留在户外，感受野生动物和繁星的时刻，这是生活中最美好的事情之一。"

但对于那些仍然希望享有一些家庭舒适的人来说，露营地是一个更合适的帐篷安营之地。在这里你可以使用洗浴设施、商店，甚至还有餐厅。如果你想要最奢华的露营体验，你也可以尝试豪华露营。在英国，露营和房车旅行一直很受欢迎。一项由英国旅游局（Visit Britain）进行的调查发现，每年大约有438万人在英国露营。

最近，由于更多人选择在英国国内度假，露营装备的销量也有所飙升。一家名为哈尔福兹（Halfords）的露营零售商报告称，诸如炉灶、冷藏箱和折叠椅等产品的需求激增。加上可充气床垫和枕头、照亮帐篷的强光手电筒和灯，以及更多易于烹饪的食物选择，你几乎可以确保一次舒适愉快的露营之旅。在英国，唯一无法保证的就是好天气！

Text B

唱歌的好处

无论你是卡拉 OK 巨星还是只在私密的淋浴间中享受歌唱的人，研究表明唱歌都能带来身心健康的好处。而且你甚至不需要擅长唱歌！

根据音乐治疗世界联合会的白沙利·穆克吉介绍，唱歌的身心优势源于多方面因素的组合。穆克吉解释说，唱歌所需要的身体努力，例如深呼吸、控制声带以及移动嘴部和身体，就是它能提升情绪的原因之一。精准地唱出每个音符需要呼吸控制和利用肺活门。这可以增加氧气摄入量和肺活量。

此外，据说集体合唱带来的好处与独唱同样众多。据估计，现在英国已经有 220 多万人定期参加合唱团。合唱团可以是业余的也可以是专业的，由擅长不同音域（如女高音或男高音）的人一起合唱，常常能营造出和谐的曲声。

2022 年维也纳大学的一项研究发现，合唱能增强群体间的信任感和凝聚力，有助于缓解抑郁和孤独。除了情绪提升，唱歌还能通过释放内啡肽（即"幸福荷尔蒙"）来降低压力和焦虑水平，这也是有明确证据的心理健康益处。

所以，无论你是否自信的歌手，都应该尝试唱歌！你不需要任何乐器，因为你就是最好的乐器。是的，你偶尔会忘词或音准有些偏离，但请记住，唱歌的好处是多方面的。

Unit 8　Humor and Happiness

Text A

Ⅰ. **Understanding the text**

1. Laughter strengthens the immune system, boosts mood, diminishes pain, protects against stress, helps release anger, facilitates forgiveness, and can even increase longevity.

2. The passage states that the ability to laugh easily and frequently is a resource for solving problems, enhancing relationships, and supporting physical and emotional health.

3. As children, we used to laugh hundreds of times a day, but as adults, laughter becomes more infrequent.

4. An essential ingredient is learning not to take ourselves too seriously and laugh at our own mistakes.

5. The ability to laugh, play, and have fun helps us think more creatively.

Ⅱ. **Vocabulary and phrases**

1. diminished　2. inspire　3. triggered　4. immune　5. burden
6. ingredient　7. diffuse　8. range　9. tension　10. alert

Ⅲ. **Translation**

1. 笑声增强免疫系统，提升情绪，减轻痛苦，并保护免受压力的伤害。
2. 没有什么比一阵爽朗的笑声更快速、更可靠地将身心重新调和。
3. 它通过消除紧张和压力放松身体，使肌肉放松长达45分钟。
4. 将更多笑声融入日常生活，无疑是一种简单而高效的改善身心状态的方式。
5. 虽然人生中一些事件确实令人悲伤，但大多数情况下，并没有强烈的悲伤或喜悦。

Ⅳ. **Writing**（略）

Text B

Ⅰ. **Understanding the text**

1. B　2. C　3. B　4. B　5. B

Ⅱ. **Translation**

1. 你每周来看我三次，持续两年，我就能治好你的恐惧症。
2. 木匠提供的简单解决方案治好了杰克的病，而费用仅为医生要价的一小部分。
3. 杰克找到了一个对他有效的、聪明的解决方案，无需支付高额的医疗费用。
4. 杰克的木匠朋友听了问题，提出了一个巧妙而经济实惠的解决方案。
5. 最终，杰克只花了10美元就得到了所需的帮助，而医生错过了一位潜在的富有客户。

参考译文
Text A

笑的力量

笑是强大的良药。这种简单的行为能够以触发身体健康的生理和情感变化的方式将人们凝聚在一起。笑声增强免疫系统，提升情绪，减轻痛苦，并保护免受压力的伤害。没有什么比一阵爽朗的笑声更快速、更可靠地将身心重新调和。

幽默轻巧地解决烦恼，激起希望，连结人与人，让我们保持专注和警觉。它还有助于发泄愤怒，促进宽恕。凭借如此强大的治愈和再生力量，拥有轻易和频繁地大笑的能力是解决问题、增进人际关系，以及维护身心健康的宝贵资源。这种无价的良药是有趣、免费且易于使用的。

笑声带来广泛而强大的好处。它通过消除紧张和压力放松身体，使肌肉放松长达 45 分钟。笑声还通过降低压力激素、增加抗感染抗体来增强免疫系统。虽然不能完全替代运动，但笑也能适度消耗热量。此外，笑声化解了愤怒和冲突，一些研究还表明它可能延长寿命。将更多笑声融入日常生活，无疑是一种简单而高效的改善身心状态的方式。

在儿童时期，我们每天都会大笑数百次，但成年后，生活变得更加严肃，笑声也更少了。但只要我们主动寻找更多幽默和欢笑的机会，就能改善情绪健康，增进人际关系，获得更多快乐，甚至可能延长寿命。

培养幽默感的关键在于不要太把自己当回事，学会对自己的错误也能大笑。虽然人生中一些事件确实令人悲伤，但大多数情况下，并没有强烈的悲伤或喜悦。所以，我们应该尽可能选择大笑。

拥有笑、玩耍和享乐的能力不仅使生活更加愉快，还有助于我们解决问题、与他人建立联系，并以更有创造力的方式思考。那些在日常生活中发现幽默的人会发现，这不仅重新激发了他们自己，也增进了所有人际关系。有了幽默，我们常常能将问题转化为创造性学习的机会。

Text B

床的问题

杰克去看医生。他有一个大问题。

"医生，"杰克说，"每次我躺在床上，我都觉得床底下有人。然后我躺到床底下，又觉得床上有人。这快把我逼疯了！"

医生说，"你每周来看我三次，持续两年，我就能治好你的恐惧症。"

"你收多少钱？"杰克问。

"每次一百美元。"医生回答。

杰克想了想。"我会考虑的。"他说。

六个月过去了，医生在街上遇到了杰克。

"你为什么再也不来看我了？"医生问。

"一次一百美元？没门！"杰克说。"我只花了 10 美元就痊愈了。"

"是吗？怎么做到的？"医生想知道。

"一个木匠帮我解决的，"杰克解释说。"他只是告诉我把床腿切掉就行了！"

木匠提供的简单解决方案治好了杰克的病，而费用仅为医生要价的一小部分。杰克找到了一个更实惠的方法来解决床的问题。

医生摇了摇头，意识到自己错过了一个轻松帮助病人的好办法。杰克找到了一个对他有效的、聪明的解决方案，无需支付高额的医疗费用。

有时候最简单的答案就是最好的。杰克的木匠朋友听了问题，提出了一个巧妙而经济实惠的解决方案。而医生则过于专注于一个漫长而昂贵的治疗计划。

最终，杰克只花了 10 美元就得到了所需的帮助，而医生错过了一位潜在的富有客户。这说明，最实际的解决方案并不总是最显而易见的。

第五部分 模拟试题参考答案

Model Test 1

Part One: Reading Comprehension (40%, 2 points each)

1. A	2. C	3. D	4. C	5. B
6. B	7. D	8. B	9. A	10. C
11. C	12. A	13. C	14. C	15. A
16. C	17. A	18. B	19. D	20. A

Part Two: Vocabulary and Structure (35%, 1 point each)

21. C	22. D	23. B	24. B	25. C
26. D	27. C	28. A	29. C	30. D
31. C	32. D	33. C	34. B	35. A
36. C	37. C	38. C	39. B	40. B
41. C	42. A	43. B	44. A	45. A
46. C	47. A	48. B	49. C	50. C
51. A	52. D	53. B	54. A	55. C

Part Three: Cloze (10%, 1 point each)

| 56. D | 57. B | 58. C | 59. B | 60. D |
| 61. A | 62. A | 63. D | 64. C | 65. B |

Part Four: Translation (15%, 3 points each)

66. 许多人相信，水果和蔬菜是他们饮食中必不可少的部分。

67. 吃多样的食物可以帮助提供我们身体所需的营养。

68. 喝足够的水对保持水分也很重要。

69. 快餐虽然方便，但通常含有过多的盐和脂肪。

70. 做出健康的选择可以带来更长久和快乐的生活。

Model Test 2

Part One: Reading Comprehension (40%, 2 points each)

1. C	2. D	3. A	4. D	5. C
6. C	7. D	8. D	9. D	10. A
11. C	12. B	13. A	14. C	15. D
16. A	17. D	18. B	19. C	20. A

Part Two: Vocabulary and Structure (35%, 1 point each)

21. B	22. A	23. D	24. D	25. A
26. D	27. B	28. D	29. B	30. A
31. C	32. C	33. A	34. B	35. A
36. B	37. C	38. C	39. A	40. C
41. A	42. A	43. D	44. B	45. D
46. A	47. C	48. A	49. B	50. C
51. D	52. D	53. D	54. D	55. A

Part Three: Cloze (10%, 1 point each)

56. D	57. C	58. B	59. C	60. D
61. A	62. D	63. A	64. B	65. B

Part Four: Translation (15%, 3 points each)

66. 读书可以提高你的词汇量和语言能力。
67. 经常阅读的人通常更能集中注意力。
68. 阅读也可以减轻压力，帮助你放松。
69. 通过书籍，你可以了解不同的文化和思想。
70. 总的来说，抽出时间阅读是一个值得培养的好习惯。

Model Test 3

Part One: Reading Comprehension (40%, 2 points each)

1. A	2. B	3. D	4. D	5. C
6. B	7. C	8. D	9. D	10. C
11. B	12. A	13. D	14. B	15. C
16. A	17. B	18. B	19. A	20. C

Part Two: Vocabulary and Structure (35%, 1 point each)

21. B	22. A	23. A	24. D	25. C
26. A	27. C	28. A	29. C	30. B
31. B	32. D	33. D	34. C	35. A
36. D	37. B	38. B	39. D	40. A
41. D	42. B	43. D	44. C	45. A
46. C	47. D	48. D	49. A	50. C
51. C	52. B	53. B	54. B	55. B

Part Three: Cloze (10%, 1 point each)

56. C	57. B	58. A	59. A	60. C
61. D	62. D	63. B	64. C	65. D

Part Four: Translation (15%, 3 points each)

66. 定期锻炼可以帮助你控制体重。
67. 它还可以增强你的肌肉和骨骼。
68. 许多研究表明，锻炼可以改善情绪，减少焦虑。
69. 你不需要在健身房待上几个小时；即使是短时间的散步也很有益。
70. 保持活跃是健康生活方式的重要部分。

Model Test 4

Part One: Reading Comprehension (40%, 2 points each)

1. A	2. C	3. B	4. C	5. B
6. B	7. B	8. C	9. A	10. D
11. A	12. C	13. A	14. C	15. D
16. A	17. D	18. C	19. D	20. B

Part Two: Vocabulary and Structure (35%, 1 point each)

21. B	22. D	23. A	24. A	25. C
26. B	27. D	28. B	29. D	30. C
31. B	32. D	33. C	34. B	35. A
36. B	37. C	38. C	39. A	40. A
41. D	42. B	43. C	44. A	45. C
46. B	47. C	48. A	49. D	50. B
51. A	52. B	53. D	54. A	55. C

Part Three: Cloze (10%, 1 point each)

56. D	57. A	58. B	59. C	60. D
61. A	62. C	63. C	64. D	65. A

Part Four: Translation (15%, 3 points each)

66. 朋友在困难时期提供支持。
67. 和朋友在一起可以带来快乐和笑声。
68. 好朋友让你感到不那么孤单，更有联系感。
69. 和朋友坦诚交流很重要。
70. 建立牢固的友谊可以改善你的整体幸福感。

参 考 文 献

［1］教育部高等学校大学外语教学指导委员会. 大学英语教学指南［M］. 北京：高等教育出版社，2020.

［2］周照兴. 从需求分析看成人高等教育英语教学［J］. 试题与研究：教学论坛，2015（23）：2.

［3］文秋芳. 构建"产出导向法"理论体系［J］. 外语教学与研究，2015，47（4）：547-558+640.

［4］王文宇. 观念、策略与英语词汇记忆［J］. 外语教学与研究，1998（1）：49-54+80.

［5］文秋芳."师生合作评价"："产出导向法"创设的新评价形式［J］. 外语界，2016（5）：37-43.

［6］杨士焯. 英汉翻译教程［M］. 北京：北京大学出版社，2006.

［7］陆谷孙. 英汉大词典［Z］. 第二版. 上海：上海译文出版社，2007.

［8］文秋芳. 输出驱动假设在大学英语教学中的应用：思考与建议［J］. 外语界，2013（6）：14-22.

［9］纪康丽. 外语学习中元认知策略的培训［J］. 外语界，2002（3）：20-26+14.

［10］杨平. 名作精译［M］. 青岛：青岛出版社，2014.